THE SOCIETY OF ILLUSTRATORS
35TH ANNUAL OF AMERICAN ILLUSTRATION
ILLUSTRATORS 35

From the exhibition held in the galleries of the
Society of Illustrators Museum of American Illustration
128 East 63rd Street, New York City
January 22 - March 26, 1993

Society of Illustrators, Inc.
128 East 63rd Street, New York, NY 10021

ISBN 0-8230-6300-3
Library of Congress Catalog Card Number 59-10849

Distributors to the trade in the United States
Watson-Guptill Publications
1515 Broadway, New York, NY 10036

Distributed throughout the rest of the world by:
Rotovision, S.A.
9 Route Suisse
1295 Mies, Switzerland

Edited by Jill Bossert
Cover design by Daniel Schwartz
Cover painting by Daniel Schwartz
Interior design by Doug Johnson and Ryuichi Minakawa
Layout and Production by Naomi Minakawa

Printed in Hong Kong

Photo Credits: C.F. Payne by Alan Brown/Photonics; Jerry Pinkney by Alan S. Orling; Elwood H. Smith by Doug
Baz; Edward Sorel by Anne Hall

ILLUSTRATORS 35

THE SOCIETY OF ILLUSTRATORS 35TH ANNUAL OF AMERICAN ILLUSTRATION

Published by Rotovision S.A. Geneva

PRESIDENT'S MESSAGE

Sincere congratulations to all those who are included in this historical edition! *Illustrators 35* continues the tradition of being the only official juried record for excellence in all facets of American illustration.

This year, we've again attempted with great determination to clearly address specific areas of illustration in order to allow an accurate representation of our profession within our Exhibition and Annual.

With the invaluable cooperation of the Chairman of our Annual Exhibition, Hodges Soileau; Assistant Chairman, Steven Stroud; and the Past Chairmen's Committee, I feel that our mission to continue this pursuit of excellence and fair representation has been superbly addressed. Thanks also go to the Publication Committee members for their efforts on behalf of our publishing ventures.

And to the students whose work was selected for our Scholarship Competition Exhibition and appears in the pages of this Annual, I send my heart-felt congratulations. Wishing you, and all illustrators everywhere, continued success and years of prosperity ahead in one of the world's finest professions.

With my warmest regards to all,

Eileen Hedy Schultz
President
1991 - 1993

Portrait by Bernie Fuchs

THE SOCIETY OF ILLUSTRATORS AWARDS: THE ILLUSTRATORS HALL OF FAME, THE HAMILTON KING AWARD, AND SPECIAL AWARDS

Since 1959, the Society of Illustrators has elected to its Hall of Fame artists recognized for their "distinguished achievement in the art of illustration." The list of previous winners is truly a "Who's Who" of illustration. Former Presidents of the Society meet annually to elect those who will be so honored.

The Hamilton King Award is presented each year for the best illustration of the year by a member of the Society of Illustrators. Selection is made by former recipients of this award.

Also, the Society of Illustrators annually presents Special Awards for substantial contributions to the profession. The Dean Cornwell Recognition Award honors someone for past service which has proven to have been an important contribution to the Society. The Arthur William Brown Achievement Award honors someone who has made a substantial contribution to the Society over a period of time. Biographies of the recipients of these awards are presented in the following pages.

HAMILTON KING AWARD 1965-1992

1965 Paul Calle	1979 William Teason
1966 Bernie Fuchs	1980 Wilson McLean
1967 Mark English	1981 Gerald McConnell
1968 Robert Peak	1982 Robert Heindel
1969 Alan E. Cober	1983 Robert M. Cunningham
1970 Ray Ameijide	1984 Braldt Bralds
1971 Miriam Schottland	1985 Attila Hejja
1972 Charles Santore	1986 Doug Johnson
1973 Dave Blossom	1987 Kinuko Y. Craft
1974 Fred Otnes	1988 James McMullan
1975 Carol Anthony	1989 Guy Billout
1976 Judith Jampel	1990 Edward Sorel
1977 Leo & Diane Dillon	1991 Brad Holland
1978 Daniel Schwartz	1992 Gary Kelley

HALL OF FAME COMMITTEE 1993

CHAIRMAN, Willis Pyle
PAST PRESIDENTS OF THE SI

Stevan Dohanos	Alvin J. Pimsler
Diane Dillon	Warren Rogers
Charles McVicker	Shannon Stirnweis
Wendell Minor	David K. Stone
Howard Munce	John Witt

HALL OF FAME LAUREATES 1958-1992

1958 Norman Rockwell	1975 Howard Pyle*	1983 Mark English	1988 Robert T. McCall
1959 Dean Cornwell	1976 John Falter	1983 Noel Sickles*	1989 Erté
1959 Harold Von Schmidt	1976 Winslow Homer*	1983 Franklin Booth*	1989 John Held Jr.*
1960 Fred Cooper	1976 Harvey Dunn*	1984 Neysa Moran McMein*	1989 Arthur Ignatius Keller*
1961 Floyd Davis	1977 Robert Peak	1984 John LaGatta*	1990 Burt Silverman
1962 Edward Wilson	1977 Wallace Morgan*	1984 James Williamson*	1990 Robert Riggs*
1963 Walter Biggs	1977 J.C. Leyendecker*	1985 Charles Marion Russell*	1990 Morton Roberts*
1964 Arthur William Brown	1978 Coby Whitmore	1985 Arthur Burdett Frost*	1991 Donald Teague
1965 Al Parker	1978 Norman Price*	1985 Robert Weaver	1991 Jessie Willcox Smith*
1966 Al Dorne	1978 Frederic Remington*	1986 Rockwell Kent*	1991 William A. Smith*
1967 Robert Fawcett	1979 Ben Stahl	1986 Al Hirschfeld	1992 Joe Bowler
1968 Peter Helck	1979 Edwin Austin Abbey*	1987 Haddon Sundblom*	1992 Edwin A. Georgi*
1969 Austin Briggs	1979 Lorraine Fox*	1987 Maurice Sendak	1992 Dorothy Hood*
1970 Rube Goldberg	1980 Saul Tepper	1988 René Bouché*	*Presented posthumously
1971 Stevan Dohanos	1980 Howard Chandler Christy*	1988 Pruett Carter*	
1972 Ray Prohaska	1980 James Montgomery Flagg*		
1973 Jon Whitcomb	1981 Stan Galli		
1974 Tom Lovell	1981 Frederic R. Gruger*		
1974 Charles Dana Gibson*	1981 John Gannam*		
1974 N.C. Wyeth*	1982 John Clymer		
1975 Bernie Fuchs	1982 Henry P. Raleigh*		
1975 Maxfield Parrish*	1982 Eric (Carl Erickson)*		

HALL OF FAME LAUREATES 1993

Robert McGinnis
Thomas Nast*
Coles Phillips*

HALL OF FAME 1993

ROBERT McGINNIS (b. 1926)

It's funny what happens with "time."

It has a curious way of passing very swiftly. No one can predict it. No one. Not even Bob McGinnis's father. Just think about this. Fifty-plus years ago he would sit around the kitchen table with little Bob and show him how to draw "Popeye." That's right, "Popeye." You see, Mr. McGinnis had a penchant for drawing cartoons and his young son, Bob, would sit around this table with the sounds of mother McGinnis, his three brothers and two sisters in the background and watch his dad draw cartoons. Bob was fascinated. His eyes would light up with wonder. He became very good at drawing "Popeye." It came easily to him. Yes, he was convinced that in time he would become a cartoonist. He must.

But, "time," when you least expect it, can play unusual tricks on you. Little did Bob or his dad suspect or predict that in time young Bob would become, not a cartoonist, but one of the most sought-after illustrators of his time. He would produce more than 1,300 paperback book covers for all the leading publishers. His 54 *Guideposts* covers are collectors' items. Many of his illustrations appeared in *The Saturday Evening Post, Good Housekeeping, Reader's Digest,* and *McCall's*, just to name a few.

But his career was not confined to publishing. When he was with Chaite Studio, sitting alongside Frank McCarthy, Bob Peak and Mike Hooks; Sam Brody, the bon vivant of fast-stepping representatives would spring into action and bring to McGinnis many an advertising assignment. He also included movie posters. Did you know Bob completed 35, plus five James Bond ads? Do you remember them? They were great. If you have any, hold on to them tight. They too are collectors' items.

Why was he so successful? I'll tell you why. I know first hand. He produced many covers for me at Bantam Books. When I commissioned him to illustrate a particular title I knew I would receive something superior to what was being done. First of all, the guy could "draw up a storm." Second, McGinnis had, and has, a superior, almost sixth sense about color. I would marvel at this aspect of his art. He had a unique way of using color by not using much color. Yet, strangely, his illustrations always appeared colorful—sensitively, selectively colorful. Obviously he had studied many of the classic, fine artists of the past and observed how they confronted the concept of color. His main medium, like the early Italian masters, has always been egg with powdered tempera.

Another unique aspect of McGinnis was that he could handle any subject. He was the complete artist. He could paint westerns, mysteries, boy-girl, science fiction...you name it, even a still life. I once amused him by giving him a still life assignment. I remember the title, *Look to the Mountain*. It was a gem. I remember when it came in. When the flap was lifted from the painting you should have heard the applause from the art department. A little jewel. I'm serious.

Anyway, the guy was a joy to work with. It was like having a dozen artists rolled into one.

Did Bob ever become a cartoonist? Yes, for a short time. When he was to graduate from high school, his teacher, Mr. Rice, was nice enough to write a rave letter of recommendation to the Disney studios. Much to the delight of Mr. McGinnis and young Bob, he was accepted and worked there for a brief time as an art apprentice. Unfortunately, World War II erupted and the studio disbanded. Bob immediately joined the Merchant Marines. (I often wondered whether "Popeye" was responsible for his going to sea.)

After his sea duty he decided to go back to school and was accepted at Ohio State, combining football and fine arts. He then enrolled at the Central Academy of Commercial Art in Cincinnati, Ohio, where he studied with the teacher who most influenced him, Mr. Gordon Jex.

Soon, and in time, Bob's work became more and more in demand. But it was Mike Hooks who was instrumental in launching Bob's vast paperback career by introducing him to Donald Gelb, Mike's rep at the time.

...And, as time continues to move along, Robert McGinnis does not get older, he just gets better and better. He is very much involved in fine art gallery painting and his highly sought-after work is held in many private collections around the country.

Way back then, sitting around that kitchen table drawing cartoons, I'm sure Mr. McGinnis would never have guessed that some day, this little kid, his son, sitting there, trying to draw "Popeye" would be elected to the prestigious Hall of Fame at the Society of Illustrators. His name would now be included with Norman Rockwell, Howard Pyle, Dean Cornwell, N.C. Wyeth, Frederic Remington...giants, all giants, and now a new giant: Robert McGinnis. He would have never guessed that. Never.

Len Leone
Former Vice President/Art Director
Bantam Books, Inc.

Portraits for cover of *The Ladies' Club*.

"The Coming of Spring," illustration for *Guideposts*, April, 1982.

HALL OF FAME 1993

THOMAS NAST (1840 - 1902)

Thomas Nast regaled the public of the mid- to late-nineteenth century with his piercing observation and unveiling of human folly, greed, and hypocrisy. His illustrations were not intended to be merely amusing, nor a result of a fleeting, impulsive dislike, but quite moralistic, a reflection of his uncompromising expectations of government and its stewards.

This surveyor of America's political system was born in Germany in 1840 and moved to New York five years later with his family. With little formal art training, Nast began to illustrate for *Frank Leslie's Illustrated News* at the age of 15, earning four dollars a week. This was the era of the wood block engraving and his drawings were not reproduced by the photochemical process until the 1880s. Between 1859 and 1887 *Harper's Weekly* was a major forum for Nast's visual polemics, a testimony to his belief in social justice, politicians' accountability to their constituency, and equitable treatment of all people, regardless of race.

By comparison to his later work, Nast's early contributions to *Harper's* are visually conservative, crowded with didactic and literal detail, and marked by an obvious concern with decorative design. The inflamed political climate of the Civil War appealed to the young artist's passions and illustrations of this era utilize a schematic mode of representation. For example, an 1863 illustration, "The Emancipation of the Negroes—the Past and the Future," presents the sufferings of the past on the left side, exhibiting the whipping, branding, and public sale of slaves, while the future is gloriously envisioned to the right, where black children gaily leave for school and a freeman enjoys the liberty of owning his own money.

The use of biblical allusion and allegorical figures typify Nast's work. In "The Union Christmas Dinner" of 1864, he equates the imagined return of the Confederacy to the Union with the return of the prodigal son to his father. Similarly, in an illustration from the following year, Nast parallels the North's victory (which to him was not just a military, but a *moral* victory) with Christ's entry into Jerusalem. One of his most powerful representations of the obstruction of Justice is seen in "Our Modern Mummy" of 1875. Here Justice represents the Supreme Court, immobilized and silenced by bandages which bind her entire body and read "Red Tape." Adding to this insult, she is so neglected that a spider has had time to weave its web from her scales.

The artist often employed literary reference—Shakespeare being one of his favorite sources—to convey a truth about 19th century political life. Horatio Seymour became victim to this form of Nastian attack when he was nominated as the Democratic presidential candidate in 1868. In addition to Nast's fundamental dislike of the Democratic Party, he was particularly disturbed by Seymour's record as Governor of New York, and was quick to revive his dishonorable role in the Draft Riots of 1863. Anticipating the politician's need to erase the incontrovertible evidence of his past wrongdoing, Nast paralleled Seymour's predicament with that of Lady Macbeth. In the cartoon, Seymour stands alone, intent upon his task and rubbing his hands which are marked "New York Riots" while the caption reads, "Out damned spot! Out I say..." Incisive, resonant and unapologetic, this is quintessential Nast.

Nast's forte of course was the bold distortion of his target's physiognomy. In the mid '60s, he began to depict his victims with heads slightly too large for their bodies, thus belittling both their appearance and their political credibility. Rotundity, thinness, long noses, and the like also became easy targets for exaggeration. William "Boss" Tweed, leader of the corrupt Tammany Hall, made frequent appearances in Nast's gallery of caricature and was eventually jailed due in large part to the illustrator's relentless campaign against his manipulation of New York's political machine. Under Nast's pen, Tweed's pear-shaped face became even longer while perfectly round and perfectly blank eyes set in circles of black created a sheep-like visage devoid of intelligence or humanity. In fact, in one of Nast's least visually complicated cartoons (sarcastically title, "The Brains"), Tweed's features are completely eliminated, replaced by a money bag stamped with a dollar sign, which sits atop his bulging corpulence, a further testament to his greed. The image is so direct that the title is almost unnecessary but sarcastically reiterates Tweed's all-consuming motivation and preoccupation: money.

In addition to his political concerns, Nast created a body of work which revealed a man who cherished goodwill, generosity, and domestic concord (the artist married Sarah Edwards in 1861 and together they had five children). The softer, more sentimental Nast was revealed every Christmas season in *Harper's*. Drawing from both European and American traditions, he created our modern version of Santa Claus: a bearded, jovial fellow who lives in the North Pole and bestows gifts to deserving children.

At the time of his death in 1902, Nast had experienced two decades of declining appreciation for his illustration. Although these years were certainly anti-climactic, the fact that his most impressive work is still heralded today is testament alone to his vision and talent.

Clare McLean

Santa Claus plate, Courtesy Thomas Nast Collection,
Macculloch Hall Historical Museum

"Seymour as Lady Macbeth," from *Harper's Weekly*

"Our Modern Mummy. Tammany Tweedledee—'She is going to punish us.'
Canal Tweedledum—'That's the best joke yet,'" from *Harper's Weekly*

HALL OF FAME 1993

COLES PHILLIPS (1880-1927)

Coles Phillips as depicted
by Norman Rockwell in 1921

Clarence Coles Phillips was the creator of that artistic mirage, the "Fade-away Girl." The progenitor for the idea occurred one night in his studio. As the artist described it, "I was lying on the studio couch and a friend was standing in front of the fire. He was fingering his violin, and the firelight shone on him in such a way that although I couldn't see anything of him except his face, the violin, shirt front, cuffs and shoes, I could tell where his arms and legs were by the way the light on his shoes and cuffs shifted. I made a quick sketch of him, then eliminated everything except his face, shirt front, cuffs and shoes. He was still there—as plain as if you had the full figure. I tried the same idea on the figure of a girl, and it seemed as if the more I took out, the easier it was to define her."

Realizing that this could be an effective picture device, he filed away the idea for some future use. That time soon came when the editors of *Life* (then the humorous weekly) wanted to inaugurate their new, full-color covers with a fresh, provocative theme. With this challenging assignment, Coles remembered the idea of the disembodied figures and decided to re-create their counterparts as a beautiful, young woman. His sister was persuaded to pose as a farm lass in a polka dot dress, scattering grain to a flock of chickens. The resulting illustration, titled "Corn Exchange," was a clever combination of visual camouflage with lost and found forms that delighted both the magazine and its readers.

Thus encouraged, the "Fade-away Girl" became a regular feature of Phillips' covers, in multitudinous variations, for nearly two decades for *Life*, *Collier's*, *Liberty*, *The Saturday Evening Post*, *Good Housekeeping*, and *Vogue* magazines.

Advertisers, too, wanted to take advantage of the popularity of Phillips' beautiful women, and he had a long affiliation with the manufacturers Holeproof Hosiery, Community Plate Silversmith, Palmolive Soap, Willys Overland (automobile) Company, and many other clients.

Phillips always drew and painted from life and his pictures required very careful prior planning. Every area was plotted out in the preliminary stages and each line or shape functioned to carry out the intended idea. Even those shapes to be omitted had to first be drawn in before determining what parts could go or stay. And, although Phillips did not always follow the fade-away formula, his pictures are always distinguished by the originality of his conceptions and his meticulously rendered designs.

"Psi" Phillips—as he was designated by his fraternity brothers at Kenyon College—always knew he wanted to be an artist and created his first published work for the yearbook and the college newspaper. Impatient to pursue his career, he left college after his Junior year and headed for New York.

There he went through a series of part-time jobs, night classes at the Chase School of Art, and a stint as a clothing catalog artist drawing herringbone patterns, buttons, or various other sartorial details in concert with an assembly line-up of other fashion artists, each adding their bit in turn.

This decidedly anonymous endeavor did not hold Psi for long, and he next graduated to an advertising agency as a sketch artist. He quickly proved his resourcefulness and learned the inner working well enough to start his own agency in 1906. However, its success took him increasingly away from the artistic side of the business, and he reluctantly decided to close up the shop and become a full-time, free-lance artist.

He talked a gullible landlord out of the first month's rent for studio space, promising that his completed work would bring a big check to pay for it. He then began to make samples of his wares. It was a pressurized learning period, but his self-defined goal was to create a picture tailored to *Life* magazine. At the end of the month, with only a single completed drawing to show, he convinced *Life*'s editor, John Ames Mitchell, of his talent and made his first sale! (And paid the landlord.)

Mitchell, who had also discovered and nurtured Charles Dana Gibson, became a life-long friend and Phillips worked for that publication regularly for many years, often doing the center double-spread or the covers.

One of his favorite early models was a young nurse from Canada, named Teresa Hyde. Their romance was a tempestuous one, but once wed, the two became a strong partnership, with Tess as the model and studio manager who kept Phillips free to work.

Because his pictures were in so much demand, he was under continual pressure to accept more commissions. In one assignment for a men's clothing catalog, he took on an impossible two months' deadline for completing all the figures in it. The resulting fee made it possible to make the down payment on a house, but the overwork may have contributed to his later ill-health.

His five-year contract to do all the monthly Fade-away Girl covers for *Good Housekeeping* proved to be more than he could handle. After two years, he had to taper off to a few covers a year. By 1924, Phillips began to suffer seriously from kidney problems, and he went abroad for a year to seek help from European specialists. None could help him, and he returned to the States unable to continue his work. His death at 47 terminated the career of an immensely popular artist with a unique ability to mesmerize and delight his appreciative audience.

Walt Reed
Illustration House

"Net Results," *Life* cover, courtesy Illustration House

HAMILTON KING AWARD 1993

JERRY PINKNEY b. 1939

From an interview with Society of Illustrators
Director Terrence Brown

Terrence Brown: Congratulations, Jerry, on the
Hamilton King. Did you think that this would be an
award you would win?

Jerry Pinkney: I have thought about the Hamilton
King Award. Whether I would ever receive it was an
open question. It's a distinguished honor because it's
awarded by one's peers. When I think of the talented
contemporaries in the jury, it makes this award
more meaningful.

TB: The piece was published by Scholastic, but
hadn't it been previously published?

JP: Yes, originally it was an assignment for *National
Geographic.* The subject was slavery and I was able to
do much of the research with the writer,
Charles Blockson.

TB: Is that subject difficult for you?

JP: It does carry deep emotions. It challenges me as a
picture maker to move beyond the anger and
frustration, to create an honest and dramatic image. I
became totally involved in black history, and the
history of slavery. Once you get past the visual
references, something takes over and that's when my
best imagery come out.

TB: The black experience has been a subject of
yours before?

JP: In the seventies there were four calendars on
African-American history for Seagrams, which
presented me with a real sense of artistic freedom.
That was a productive time in my career, both
personally and professionally. And, of course, there
were the nine U.S. Postal issues for the Black
Heritage Series.

TB: We all have Steve Dohanos to thank for the
Citizen Stamp Advisory Committee's appreciation
of illustration.

JP: Yes, he brought the illustrator's point of view to
that committee. Also, I saw those assignments from a
design point of view. I was proud to have been a part
of the Committee ten years.

TB: Your early background was more in design than
illustration, wasn't it?

JP: I was a Design major at the Philadelphia College
of Art and did more design than illustration at
Russcraft Publishing Company in Boston those first
years out of school.

TB: Was the distance from New York at that time
a hindrance?

JP: Not entirely, since my agent, Cullen Rapp, was
representing me in New York. And I made a point to
see the shows and follow the trades.

TB: How do you feel about your earlier work?

JP: I am amazed at the diversity of it then, and by
how far I have come...how much my style had grown.

TB: And growth is important?

JP: I'm always looking inside to see if I can push
myself further. I look at other artists to see their
growth and to see parallels in our work, but never to
just follow trends. There is more freedom outside

trends to develop one's personal style.

TB: Today, you are a star in the children's book field.
What was your development in this market?

JP: I illustrated my first book in 1964. It's still in print
and the modest royalty each year still amazes me. *The
Patchwork Quilt,* in 1984, was my first book in color.
But as an artist active in other markets, I was not at
the top of many publisher's lists in the seventies. Atha
Tehon at Dial Books for Young Readers was the first
to encourage me. She had the insight to nurture
my talents.

TB: The children's book market has changed
dramatically in recent years.

JP: I was fortunate to have had an audience for my
books when it changed. I was in the right place at the
right time.

TB: What do you see as the uniqueness of this market?

JP: You know your audience: children, parents,
teachers, and librarians. It is a market where your
work has longevity. There is always a new audience to
replace young readers who move on to another lever.
A book can become a classic and be around for many
years. Think of such artists as Howard Pyle, N.C.
Wyeth, and Maurice Sendak.

TB: Do you work well with the text and the designers?

JP: My design and production experience comes into
play when working with editors and art directors on
designing the rhythm and format of a book. It is
important, however, for both the text and the art to
provide an open image for the reader.

TB: It is certainly a market well covered by the media.

JP: It does have its awards, shows, and lists, but they
have different audiences in themselves. *The New York
Times* Ten Best Children's Books speaks of aesthetics.
The Caldecott, which is so well known publicly, is
awarded by the American Library Association. And,
there is the Golden Kite Award given by The Society
of Children's Book Writers and Illustrators, and
others such as the AIGA Book Show.

TB: And the Society's juried show, "The Original Art"?

JP: "The Original Art" show is juried by people
sensitive to children's book illustration. I see its
purpose as raising expectations. All of the shows and
awards should serve to inspire us to the extraordinary.

TB: Your family is now grown and your wife, Gloria
Jean, has begun a writing career. Also, Brian, your
oldest son, is a children's book illustrator. And
Andrea, his wife, is a writer.

JP: It's an exciting time for the Pinkney family. You
can imagine the energetic conversation when
we're together.

TB: Do you see yourself in the children's book market
in the years ahead?

JP: Yes, the publishers are giving me exciting projects.
My career is in the right direction...it is limitless.
However, I don't rule out important projects like the
recent *National Geographic* story on the slave trade in
Brazil in the 17th century. That subject was very
emotional but one I wanted. And, there was the
Land's End catalogue cover-these departures are
good for me.

TB: And your personal work?

JP: I came into this business to be an illustrator.
I would like to develop my own ideas with writers.
As an artist, I am always challenging myself...I am
going "out on a limb," or let's say, "I'm creeping out
on a limb."

Hamilton King Award winner, jacket illustration for
"GET ON BOARD, *The Story of the Underground Railroad*"
commissioned by Scholastic Inc.

SPECIAL AWARDS 1993

1993 Dean Cornwell Recognition Award
ROBERT GEISSMANN

Bob Geissmann, who was my good and trusted friend, loved to show off his ability to do one handed push-ups, no matter what his condition. He dressed as a Brooks Brothers artist might, a perfect Rob Roy was his drink, and a good party his game. His fuse could be short at times, but his endless capacity to help and to lead were his long suits.

It was natural for Geissmann, with his great talent and charm, to gravitate to the Society of Illustrators. From the first day of his membership in the Society, through his presidency from 1953 to 1955, to his last day, Geissmann served the Society to the best of his ability. His vision for the Society was total professionalism first, party second—he never lost sight of that vision. He always strove to make the Society and our profession better and he backed up his vision and goals with his brains and brawn.

Geissmann's deep concern for professional standards and practices was felt not only at the Society, but also in his involvement at the Graphic Artists Guild, an organization Bob helped to form, becoming their first president in 1969. His interest in the ethical standards then being practiced in the illustration profession during the late '40s and the concern by members of the Society, the Art Directors Club and the Artists Guild, led to the founding of the Joint Ethics Committee in 1945 and their formulation of the Code of Fair Practice.

Through contacts made during World War II, Geissmann was the driving force behind the Society's participation in the U.S. Air Force Art Program, which was conceived by Lt. Col. Bill Lookadoo and implemented by Lt. Col. George C. Bales. Bob chaired the committee, with John Moodie, from 1954 to 1958.

Geissmann's participation in and enthusiasm for the Society's annual theatrical presentations was legendary. He often helped to write the show, organize the backstage activities, cast for the dancers and, of course, perform center stage.

For Bob Geissmann, there were no unimportant jobs at the Society. He tackled each task as if the very existence of the Society depended on the job being done on time and to perfection. He would have been flattered and very honored to have received this award from his peers.

Jerry McConnell
House Chairman

1993 Arthur William Brown Achievement Award
WALTER HORTENS

A gentle and kind man, rather courtly and refined of manner, reflective perhaps of his Viennese birthplace, Walter Hortens joined the Society in 1958 and thus began an association which was to continue for thirty years until his death in 1988.

He studied at Pratt Institute in New York and at the Academie Julian in Paris with Fernand Léger. An inveterate traveler, his fluency in German, French, and Italian served him well. Characteristically, his involvement with the Society touched many areas, as he was always willing to pitch in where needed. His service included many years as a member of the Board of Directors, as the Society's representative on the Joint Ethics Committee, and as the instigator of the Society's participation in the Police Athletic League's program for New York's disadvantaged youth. Walter's participation at the Society culminated in a two-term presidency from 1985 to 1987.

Soft spoken, acutely considerate in his personal relations, and generous in sharing information with colleagues, Walter's rather benign demeanor masked a steely, even obstinate, determination to rectify many of the injustices found in our profession. Many pay lip service to artists' rights, but Walter had the courage of his convictions and was willing to take on substantial clients in confrontations over issues in dispute, *The New York Times* among them, and to persevere until he won. He knew full well the price to be paid for winning.

Possessed of a sly sense of humor, Walter noted at the President's Dinner, which marked the termination of his term and the election of the Society's first woman President, Diane Dillon, that it was the first time in the Society's 75-year history that the outgoing President and the incoming President had kissed.

Surely if anyone epitomizes the spirit and intent of The Arthur William Brown Achievement Award for many years of service to the Society, it is Walter Hortens.

Dean Ellis
Treasurer

CHAIRMAN'S MESSAGE

The most important ingredient for an outstanding Annual Exhibition is the selection of good juries—all 36 jurors were diligent and conscientious in their deliberations. The relationship of quality of work to quality of jury is evident in the eclectic body of work in this Annual. We are grateful to those responsible for such excellence.

If anyone had suggested that I might someday have the honor of chairing the Annual Exhibition, an event which has meant so much to me and so many other illustrators, I would never have believed it. This is, in my opinion, the most important exhibition of illustration in which anyone can participate. For this reason, I'm extremely proud of the result of this year's effort.

Many dedicated people generously donated their time to make this ambitious undertaking a success. Without their support, it would have been difficult, if not impossible. Many thanks to Eileen Hedy Schultz and Terry Brown and the SI staff: Phyllis, Clare, Mike, Dan, Babe, and Jill. I'd also like to thank my assistant, Steve Stroud, for setting a new standard for the job of Assistant Chairman. He made this challenge easier, but most of all, fun.

Glenn Harrington, one of the many young lions of illustration, created an evocative image for the Call for Entry. Doug Johnson took that image and designed a terrific poster.

Congratulations to all the award winners and to all those who are included in this Annual. This really is quite an elite group when one considers, of nearly 7,000 entires, fewer than 500 were selected. Thank you all for making this a special book.

If the work in this book is any indication, illustration is certainly alive and well.

Hodges Soileau
Chairman, 35th Annual Exhibition

Portrait by Bernie Fuchs

EDITORIAL JURY

WILSON McLEAN
CHAIRMAN
Illustrator

GIL COHEN
Artist/Illustrator

JEFF CORNELL
Illustrator

NORMAN S. HOTZ
Senior Art Editor
Reader's Digest Magazine

BOB LAPSLEY
Illustrator

JIM PLUMERI
Executive Art Director
Bantam Doubleday Dell

MARK SUMMERS
Illustrator

LYNN SWEAT
Illustrator

KENT WILLIAMS
Illustrator

EDITORIAL

AWARD WINNERS

JERRY PINKNEY
Gold Medal

SKIP LIEPKE
Silver Medal

C.F. PAYNE
Silver Medal

JANET WOOLLEY
Silver Medal

1

Artist: **JERRY PINKNEY**

Art Director: Allen Carroll

Client: National Geographic

Size: 15 x 20 1/4

JERRY PINKNEY
Editorial Gold Medal

"This painting, "Survivor for Sale, The Scramble Auction," was one of the most challenging illustrations of my career, not only because of the research, but also because of the assumptions one has to make with subject matter that has little documentation. Most of all, one feels the emotional demands when dealing as honestly as possible with a history that has so much pain and degradation attached to it. My intent was to show the fear, confusion, and disorientation of the Africans and at the same time convey a sense of resistance to a dehumanizing experience."

Artist: **SKIP LIEPKE**

Art Director: Fred Woodward

Client: Rolling Stone

Medium: Oil

Size: 21 ¹/₂ x 14 ¹/₂

SKIP LIEPKE
Editorial Silver Medal

"The Bob Dylan piece was pretty straightforward (as I guess all my work is). I just tried to tap into something that moved me about him, something I hope others can see and feel. It's hard for me to speak eloquently about something that was far better expressed in paint. Without getting too verbose, I guess what I do is paint people, and what I say about them is as open as the human experience."

3

Artist: **C. F. PAYNE**

Art Director: Joseph Connolly

Client: Boys' Life

Size: 13 x 26

C.F. PAYNE
Editorial Silver Medal

"This project was a departure for me and one I looked upon with excitement and great expectations. Then what followed was not expected. Doing a project on a significant figure in a major moment in history was thrilling and a new challenge, but the subject matter regarding this figure had an unexpected effect on me. I was not anticipating those feelings, nor was I prepared. Yet I am proud of the illustration that was produced. I am also proud of *Boys' Life*'s willingness to take on such a subject for their magazine and for giving me this assignment."

4

Artist: **JANET WOOLLEY**

Art Director: Fred Woodward

Client: Rolling Stone

Size: 19 x 16

JANET WOOLLEY
Editorial Silver Medal

"I was born in Plymouth, England, in 1952. After attending Shrewsbury School of Art until 1970, I went to Brighton College of Art and Design, leaving in 1973 with a B.A. Honors Degree in Graphic Design. Between 1973 and 1976, I attended the Royal College of Art, where I received the Berger Sword for Drawing and a Master of Arts Degree in Illustration. Among the awards I have won are Sainsbury Image of Today, Benson & Hedges Gold, and the Society of Illustrators' Gold and Silver Medals. I have worked mainly in the area of illustration in the U.K. and the U.S.A. and I also lecture at Central Saint Martins School of Art in London."

5

Artist: **MARSHALL ARISMAN**

Art Director: Charmian Carl

Client: Playgirl Magazine

Medium: Oil

Size: 38 x 38

6

Artist: **MARSHALL ARISMAN**

Art Director: Rhonda Rubinstein

Client: Esquire

7

Artist: **STEVE BRODNER**

Art Directors: Jill Armus

Client: Total TV

Medium: Watercolor

Size: 10 1/2 x 16

8

Artist: **KEITH GRAVES**

Art Director: D. J. Stout

Client: Texas Monthly

Medium: Prisma color

Size: 13 x 10

9

Artist: **DAVID M. BECK**

Art Director: Saroyan Humphrey

Client: Guitar Player Magazine

Medium: Mixed media

Size: 16 x 12

5

7

8

9

10

Artist: **ALAN E. COBER**

Art Director: Ron Arnholm

Client: Georgia Review

Medium: Etching, aquatint

Size: 31 x 22

11

Artist: **DAVE CUTLER**

Art Director: A. J. Hartley

Client: The Detroit Free Press

Medium: Acrylic on paper

Size: 16 x 20

12

Artist: **JACK UNRUH**

Art Director: Fred Woodward

Client: Rolling Stone

Size: 14 x 10

13

Artist: **PHIL BOATWRIGHT**

Art Director: Christine Mitchell

Client: Arizona Highways
Magazine

Medium: Mixed media

Size: 16 x 12

14

Artist: **GLENN HARRINGTON**

Art Directors: Pam Powers
Ron Ramsey

Client: Golf Magazine

Size: 15 x 20

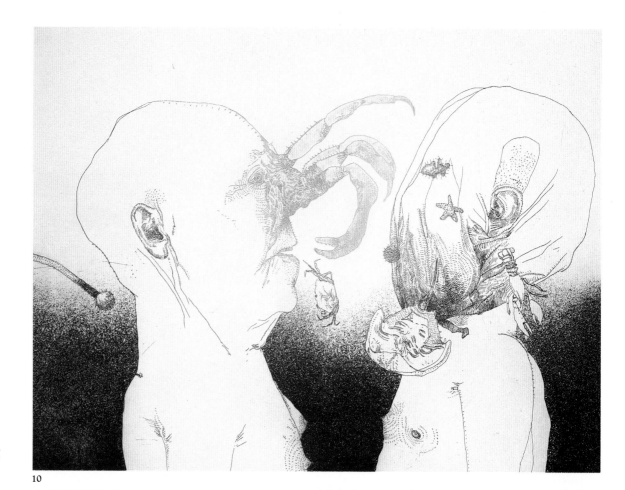

10

11

12

13

14

15

Artist: **KINUKO Y. CRAFT**

Art Director: Kerig Pope

Client: Playboy

Size: 15 x 15 ¹/₂

16

Artist: **ROBERT GIUSTI**

Art Director: Kerig Pope

Client: Playboy

Size: 10 x 10

17

Artist: **BRAD HOLLAND**

Art Director: Hans-Georg Pospischil

Client: FAZ GmbH

Medium: Acrylic on board

Size: 19 x 25

18

Artist: **RALPH STEADMAN**

Art Directors: Michael Grossman
Gregory Mastrianni

Client: Entertainment Weekly

19

Artist: **CHARLES S. PYLE**

Art Director: Rhonda Rubinstein

Client: Esquire

15

16

17

18

19

20

Artist: **DAVE CUTLER**

Art Director: Meg Birnbaum

Client: Natural Health

Medium: Acrylic on paper

Size: 6 ¹/₂ x 5 ¹/₂

21

Artist: **JOHN LABBÉ**

Art Director: A. J. Harrey

Client: The Detroit Free Press

Size: 15 ¹/₂ x 18

22

Artist: **H. B. LEWIS**

Art Director: Karen Siciliano

Client: The Wall Street Journal
Classroom

Medium: Mixed media

Size: 10 x 17

23

Artist: **RICH BOWMAN**

Art Director: Tom Dolphens

Client: Kansas City Star

Medium: Oil

Size: 17 ¹/₂ x 13

24

Artist: **SUN-KYUNG CHO**

Size: 16 x 12

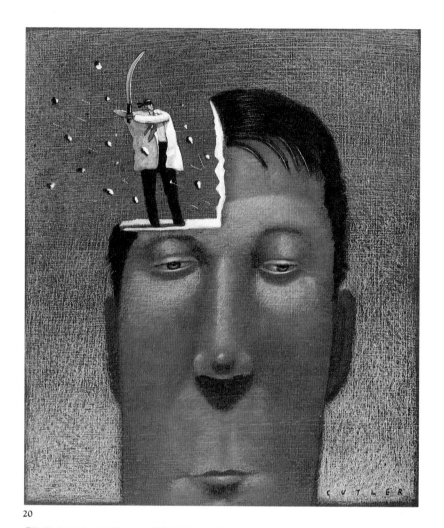

20

21

22

23

24

25

Artist: **JIM SPANFELLER**

Art Directors: Tom Staebler
Kerig Pope

Client: Playboy

Medium: Mixed media

Size: 16 x 16

26

Artist: **JIM SPANFELLER**

Art Director: Robert I. York

Client: Spanfeller Graphics
Group, Inc.

Size: 28 x 30

27

Artist: **HERBERT TAUSS**

Art Director: Allen Carroll

Client: National Geographic

Medium: Oil

Size: 39 x 54

28

Artist: **DAVID JOHNSON**

Art Director: Mindy Phelps Stanton

Client: Times Mirror Magazines

Medium: Watercolor, ink

Size: 12 x 24

29

Artist: **GREG SPALENKA**

Art Director: Elaine Bradley

Client: Vermont Magazine

Medium: Mixed media

Size: 8 x 13

25

27

28

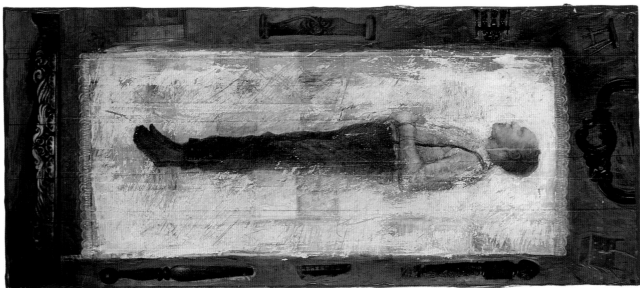

29

30

Artist: **KINUKO Y. CRAFT**

Art Director: Rhonda Kass

Client: Forbes

Size: 17 1/2 x 12 1/2

31

Artist: **C. MICHAEL DUDASH**

Art Directors: John Fennell
C. Michael Dudash

Client: Step-By-Step Graphics

Medium: Oil on linen/paper

Size: 24 x 17

32

Artist: **C. MICHAEL DUDASH**

Art Directors: Gary Kelley
C. Michael Dudash

Client: The North American
Review

Medium: Oil on linen/paper

Size: 35 x 27

33

Artist: **GREGORY MANCHESS**

Art Director: Steve Connatser

Client: "D" Magazine

Medium: Oil

Size: 14 x 25

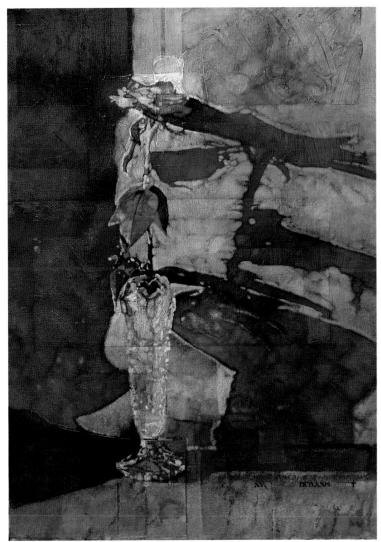

31

32

33

34

Artist: **JOHN COLLIER**

Art Director: Fred Woodward

Client: Rolling Stone

Medium: Pastel

Size: 26 x 21

35

Artist: **BILL NELSON**

Art Directors: Deborah Flynn-
      Hanvahan
      Robin Gilmore-
      Barnes

Client: The Atlantic Monthly

Medium: Colored pencil

Size: 5 x 12

36

Artist: **MATT MAHURIN**

Client: Houston Metropolitan
      Magazine

Size: 13 x 10

37

Artist: **GREG SPALENKA**

Art Director: Nancy Duckworth

Client: The Los Angeles Times
      Magazine

Medium: Mixed media

Size: 16 1/2 x 12 1/2

34

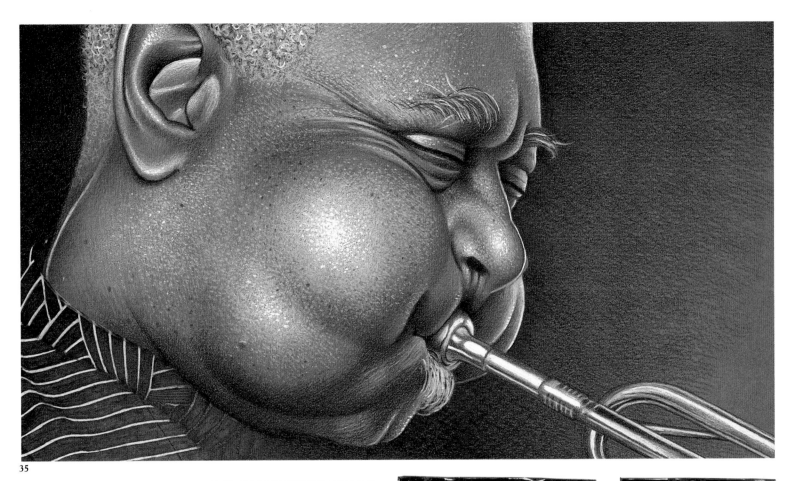

35

36

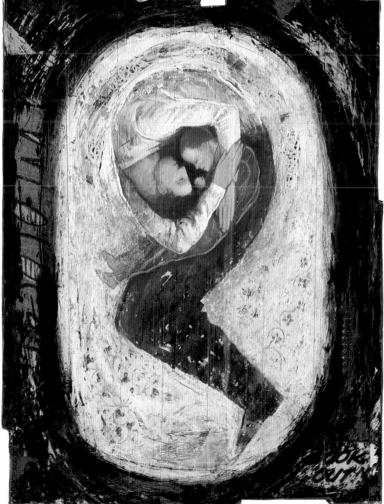

37

38

Artist: **BLAIR DRAWSON**

Art Director: Fred Woodward

Client: Rolling Stone

Size: 12 x 10 1/4

39

Artist: **ALAN E. COBER**

Art Director: Fred Woodward

Client: Rolling Stone

Size: 9 x 7 1/2

40

Artist: **SKIP LIEPKE**

Client: Eleanor Ettinger Inc.

Medium: Watercolor

Size: 13 1/2 x 9 1/2

41

Artist: **KUNIO HAGIO**

Art Director: Richard Bleiweiss

Client: Penthouse

Medium: Oil

Size: 24 x 18

42

Artist: **SALLY WERN COMPORT**

Art Director: Roy Comiskey

Client: Security Management

Medium: Mixed media

Size: 17 x 13

38

39

40

41

42

43

Artist: **KINUKO Y. CRAFT**

Art Director: Tom Staebler

Client: Playboy

Medium: Egg tempera

Size: 18 x 16

44

Artist: **JAMES CHAFFEE**

Medium: Pen, ink, watercolor

Size: 19 x 19

45

Artist: **JOHN JUDE PALENCAR**

Art Director: J. Porter

Client: Yankee Magazine

Size: 12 x 19

46

Artist: **ERIC DINYER**

Medium: Macintosh Quadra 950

Size: 11 x 8 1/2

47

Artist: **ADAM NIKLEWICZ**

Art Directors: Judy Garlan
Robin Gilmore-Barnes

Client: The Atlantic Monthly

Medium: Acrylic on illustration board

Size: 8 x 6

43

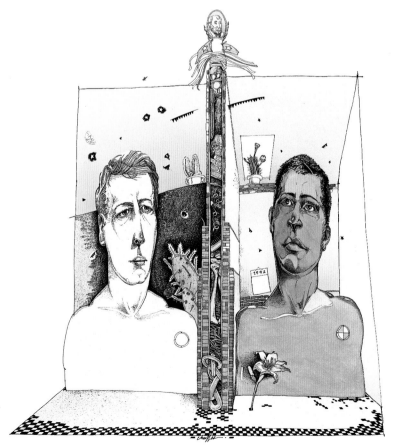

44

45

46

47

48

Artist: **PHIL BOATWRIGHT**

Art Director: Larry Stuart

Client: Discipleship Journal

Medium: Mixed media

Size: 20 x 16 ¹/₂

49

Artist: **KATHERINE LANDIKUSIC**

Art Director: Tom Dolphens

Client: The Kansas City Star

Size: 16 x 23

50

Artist: **PHIL BOATWRIGHT**

Art Director: Christine Mitchell

Client: Arizona Highways Magazine

Medium: Mixed media

Size: 16 x 12

51

Artist: **TIM O'BRIEN**

Medium: Oil on gessoed panel

Size: 18 x 11 ³/₄

49

50

51

52

Artist: **JOEL PETER JOHNSON**

Art Director: Mark Geer

Client: Caring Magazine

Medium: Mixed media

Size: 7 1/2 x 7 3/4

53

Artist: **WILSON McLEAN**

Art Director: Richard Bleiweiss

Client: Penthouse

Medium: Oil

Size: 21 x 23

54

Artist: **PETER FIORE**

Art Director: Roger Dowd

Client: Medical Economics

Medium: Oil

Size: 30 x 20

55

Artist: **MATT MAHURIN**

Art Director: Jane Palecek

Client: Health Magazine

Size: 13 x 10

56

Artist: **MATT MAHURIN**

Art Director: Sandy Chellisto

Client: The Los Angeles Times

Size: 10 x 13 1/4

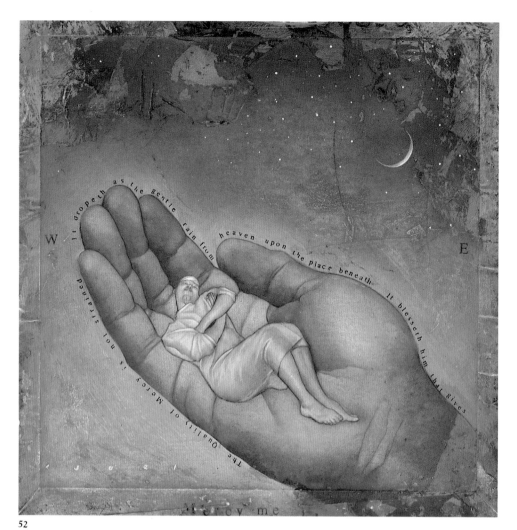

52

53

54

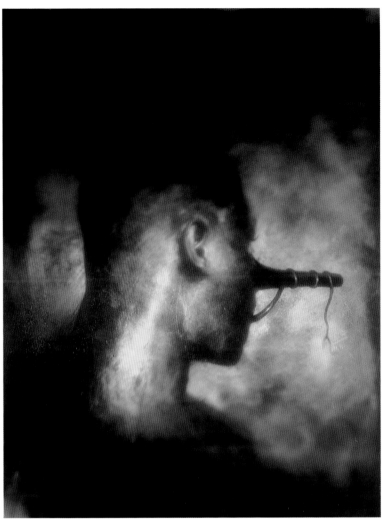

55

56

57

Artist: **ELWOOD H. SMITH**

Art Directors: Kelly Doe
Richard Baker

Client: The Washington Post
Magazine

Medium: Watercolor, india ink

Size: 11 x 10 1/2

58

Artist: **DAVID JOHNSON**

Art Director: John Korpics

Client: Musician Magazine

Medium: Pen, ink, watercolor

Size: 10 1/2 x 9 1/2

59

Artist: **PETER DE SÈVE**

Art Director: Bob Mansfield

Client: Forbes

Size: 12 3/4 x 9

60

Artist: **JOHN P. MAGGARD III**

Art Director: Simon Smith

Client: American Legion Magazine

Medium: Acrylic, oil

Size: 23 x 17

61

Artist: **WM. A. MOTTA**

Art Director: Richard M. Baron

Client: Road & Track Magazine

Size: 24 x 26

57

58

59

60

61

62

Artist: **JOHN THOMPSON**

Art Director: Tom Staebler

Client: Playboy

Medium: Oil

Size: 18 x 17

63

Artist: **JANET WOOLLEY**

Art Director: Michael Grossman

Client: Entertainment Weekly

Size: 20 x 16

64

Artist: **C. F. PAYNE**

Art Director: Richard Bleiweiss

Client: Penthouse

Medium: Mixed media

Size: 16 x 20

65

Artist: **DANIEL SCHWARTZ**

Art Director: Fred Woodward

Client: Rolling Stone

Medium: Oil

Size: 13 x 10 1/2

66

Artist: **WIKTOR SADOWSKI**

Art Director: Fred Woodward

Client: Rolling Stone

Size: 15 x 12 1/2

62

63

64

65

66

67

Artist: **BRALDT BRALDS**

Art Director: Fred Woodward

Client: Rolling Stone

Size: 12 x 10

68

Artist: **JOE CIARDIELLO**

Art Director: Tim Pedersen

Client: Jazziz

Medium: Ink, watercolor

Size: 13 x 10

69

Artist: **BRAD HOLLAND**

Art Director: Fred Woodward

Client: Rolling Stone

Size: 12 x 10

70

Artist: **CHRISTOPHER A. KLEIN**

Art Director: Mark Holmes

Client: National Geographic

Medium: Acrylic

Size: 21 x 11

71

Artist: **JOSEPH DANIEL FIEDLER**

Art Director: Lucy Bartholomay

Client: The Boston Globe Magazine

Medium: Alkyd on paper

Size: 16 x 13 1/4

67

69

70

71

72

Artist: **HERB DAVIDSON**

Art Director: Tom Staebler

Client: Playboy

Medium: Oil

Size: 24 x 20

73

Artist: **MARK SUMMERS**

Art Director: Steve Heller

Client: The New York Times
Book Review

Medium: Scratchboard

Size: 7 x 4 3/4

74

Artist: **JOHN COLLIER**

Art Director: Fred Woodward

Client: Rolling Stone

Medium: Pastel

Size: 36 x 24

75

Artist: **ARTHUR SHILSTONE**

Art Director: Caroline Despard

Client: Smithsonian Magazine

Medium: Watercolor

Size: 19 3/4 x 28 1/4

72

73

74

75

76

Artist: **C. F. PAYNE**

Art Director: Sokie Gonzales

Client: U.S. News & World Report

Medium: Mixed media

Size: 15 x 12

77

Artist: **JERRY PINKNEY**

Art Director: Allen Carroll

Client: National Geographic

Size: 14 3/4 x 20

78

Artist: **GARY KELLEY**

Art Director: Martha Geering

Client: Sierra Magazine

Medium: Pastel

Size: 15 x 12 1/2

79

Artist: **BLAIR DRAWSON**

Art Director: Rhonda Rubinstein

Client: Esquire

Size: 15 x 12 1/2

76

77

78

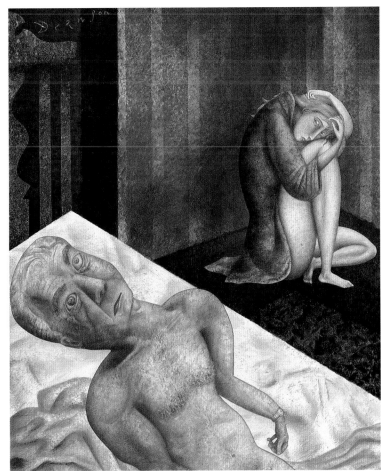

79

80

Artist: **JACK UNRUH**

Art Director: Allen Carroll

Client: National Geographic

Medium: Pen, ink, watercolor

Size: 21 1/2 x 21 1/2

81

Artist: **DAVID WILCOX**

Art Directors: Kerig Pope
            Kelly Korjenek

Client: Playboy

Medium: Casein

Size: 21 x 21

82

Artist: **DON WELLER**

Art Director: Don Weller

Client: Park City Lodestar
      Magazine

Medium: Plastic overlay

Size: 11 x 15

83

Artist: **MEL ODOM**

Art Director: Tom Staebler

Client: Playboy

Medium: Airbrush, colored pencil

Size: 10 x 7 1/2

84

Artist: **BILL NELSON**

Art Director: Fred Woodward

Client: Rolling Stone

Medium: Colored pencil

Size: 16 x 14

80

81

82

83

84

85

Artist: **BURT SILVERMAN**

Art Director: Peter Morance

Client: American Heritage

Size: 30 x 24

86

Artist: **ROB WOOD**

Art Director: Wayne Fitzpatrick

Client: U.S. News & World Report

Size: 14 x 11

87

Artist: **JOHN RUSH**

Art Director: Tom Staebler

Client: Playboy

Medium: Oil

Size: 31 x 21

88

Artist: **RICHARD SCHLECHT**

Art Director: Allen Carroll

Client: National Geographic

Medium: Watercolor

Size: 19 x 26

85

86

87

88

89

Artist: **DOUGLAS C. KLAUBA**

Art Director: Anthony Ficke

Client: Pension & Investment
Magazine

Medium: Acrylic

Size: 21 x 16

90

Artist: **CAROLE KABRIN**

Art Director: Katherine Dillon

Client: ABC News

Medium: Pastel

Size: 15 1/2 x 18 1/2

91

Artist: **DANIEL MAFFIA**

Art Director: Fred Woodward

Client: Rolling Stone

Size: 16 1/2 x 14

92

Artist: **MARVIN MATTELSON**

Art Director: Richard Bleiweiss

Client: Penthouse

Medium: Acrylic

Size: 13 x 10

93

Artist: **ARTHUR SHILSTONE**

Art Director: Mindy Phelps Stanton

Client: Times Mirror Magazines

Medium: Watercolor

Size: 13 x 15

89

90

91

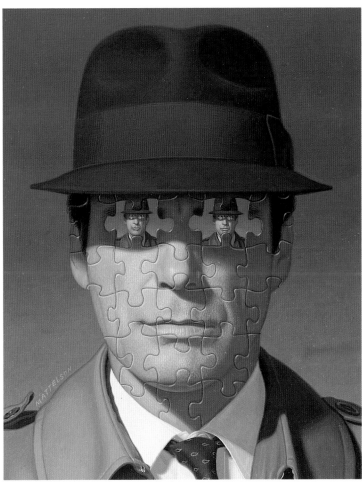

92

93

94

Artist: **MARSHALL ARISMAN**

Art Director: Alfred Zelser

Client: Men's Health

Size: 29 x 23

95

Artist: **WILSON McLEAN**

Art Director: Tom Staebler

Client: Playboy

Medium: Acrylic on canvas

Size: 21 x 25

96

Artist: **JIM PHALEN**

Medium: Oil on board

Size: 18 x 15

97

Artist: **JOHN LABBÉ**

Art Directors: Nicholas E. Torello
Joy Toltzis Makon

Client: Scholastic Inc.

Size: 17 1/2 x 14

94

95

96

97

98

Artist: **C. F. PAYNE**

Art Director: D.J. Stout

Client: Texas Monthly

Medium: Mixed media

Size: 15 x 12

99

Artist: **GUY BILLOUT**

Art Director: Jan Zimmeck

Client: Kiplinger's Personal
Finance

Medium: Watercolor, airbrush

Size: 11 1/8 x 16 1/4

100

Artist: **BURT SILVERMAN**

Art Directors: Nick Kirilloff
Allen Carroll

Client: National Geographic

Medium: Oil

Size: 20 x 18 1/2

101

Artist: **MARK SUMMERS**

Art Director: Steve Heller

Client: The New York Times
Book Review

Medium: Scratchboard

Size: 8 x 7 1/4

99

100

101

102

Artist: **SKIP LIEPKE**

Client: Eleanor Ettinger Inc.

Medium: Watercolor

Size: 9 x 12

103

Artist: **SKIP LIEPKE**

Client: Eleanor Ettinger Inc.

Medium: Oil

Size: 12 x 16

104

Artist: **TOM WOODRUFF**

Art Director: Fred Woodward

Client: Rolling Stone

Size: 24 x 19

105

Artist: **FRED OTNES**

Art Director: Jane Polanka

Client: National Academy of
Science

Medium: Mixed-media collage

Size: 25 x 37

102

103

104

105

106

Artist: **JERRY PINKNEY**

Art Director: Allen Carroll

Client: National Geographic

Size: 14 x 9 3/4

107

Artist: **BRAD HOLLAND**

Art Director: Hans-Georg Pospischil

Client: FAZ GmbH

Medium: Acrylic on board

Size: 18 1/2 x 25 1/2

108

Artist: **JOHN MARTIN**

Art Director: Nicole White

Client: Network Computing
   Magazine

Medium: Acrylic

Size: 23 x 17

109

Artist: **EVANGELIA
   PHILLIPPIDIS**

Art Director: Bob James

Client: The Columbus Dispatch

Size: 15 x 10 1/2

106

107

108

109

110

Artist: **GARNET HENDERSON**

Art Director: Carol Carson

Client: Scholastic Inc.

111

Artist: **KENNETH FRANCIS DEWEY**

Art Director: Dan Hayward

Client: Pennysaver

Medium: Pen, ink,watercolor

Size: 22 x 30

112

Artist: **ARTHUR SHILSTONE**

Art Director: Gary Gretter

Client: Sports Afield

Size: 16 x 11

113

Artist: **ELWOOD H. SMITH**

Art Directors: Robert Lascaro
        Matthew Fernberger

Client: Scholastic Inc.

Size: 12 1/2 x 9

114

Artist: **MARK BELLEROSE**

Art Directors: Nancy Stetler
        Irene Pombo

Client: Patient Care Magazine

Medium: Pastel

Size: 9 x 6 1/2

111

113

112

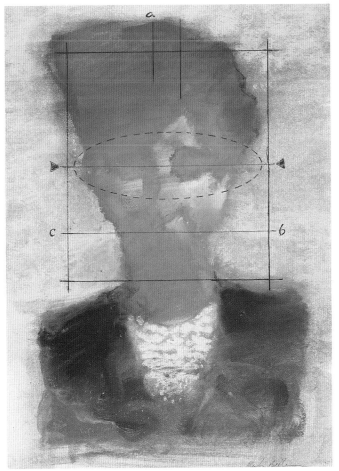

114

BOOK JURY

PETER FIORE
CHAIRMAN
Illustrator

ED ACUÑA
Illustrator

TOM DEMETER
Senior Creative Director
Blazing Graphics

ELAINE DUILLO
Illustrator

LOIS ERLACHER
Art Director
Emergency Medicine Magazine

LEONARD P. LEONE
Designer/Artist/Illustrator

ROBERT E. McGINNIS
Illustrator

NEIL McPHEETERS
Illustrator

STEVEN STROUD
Illustrator

BOOK

AWARD WINNERS

STEVE JOHNSON/LOU FANCHER
Gold Medal

BRYAN LEISTER
Gold Medal

GENNADY SPIRIN
Gold Medal

GARY KELLEY
Silver Medal

JERRY PINKNEY
Silver Medal

SAELIG GALLAGHER
Silver Medal

115

Artists: **STEVE JOHNSON/
LOU FANCHER**

Art Director: Lou Fancher

Client: Lothrop Lee & Shepard
Books

Medium: Acrylic on paper

Size: 12 ³/4 x 10 ¹/2

STEVE JOHNSON/LOU FANCHER
Book Gold Medal

Working as a collaborative team, Steve Johnson and Lou Fancher have
spent the last six years producing illustrations for magazines, annual
reports, posters, advertisements, and children's books. Because their
process is unusual—each painting is created through a back-and-forth
joint effort—they've sometimes struggled to explain how they work.
Steve says, "You'd have to sit right next to us and watch, which would
be pretty tedious, but working together means the ideas and the
paintings are better. After six years, I don't think either of us can
imagine working without the other person." This painting is from their
fourth children's book, *Up North at the Cabin.*

116

Artist: **BRYAN LEISTER**

Art Director: Doris Borowsky-Straus

Client: St. Martin's Press

Medium: Oil

Size: 14 1/2 x 10

BRYAN LEISTER
Book Gold Medal

"This painting was done for a book about a plot to assassinate Queen Elizabeth. The assassin was to hide in the eye of a gigantic dragon float. Doris Borowsky-Straus, the art director, had come up with this idea of the Queen with the dragon in her lap. I had just seen Leonardo's "Lady with an Ermine" at the National Gallery in Washington, D.C., which inspired me to render the dragon in this pose. I combined several versions of the Queen's portrait in order to come up with the most ideal."

Art Directors: Atha Tehon
Amelia Lau Carling

Client: Dial Books for Young
Readers

Medium: Watercolor

Size: 8 1/2 x 15

Spirin, a native of Moscow and product of the Russian art education system, which recognizes special talents and trains children at an early age, began his career in the former Soviet Union. He moved to the U.S. for a six-month visit but enjoyed the conditions and remained. Of his work he said, "*Snow White and Rose Red* is a classic tale by the brothers Grimm. It is a story I loved as a child, set in a part of Northern Europe that is very familiar to me. There are many dramatic, magical incidents that lent themselves to my style."

118

Artist: **GARY KELLEY**

Art Directors: Tom Peterson
             Louise Fili

Client: Creative Education

Medium: Pastel

Size: 19 x 12

GARY KELLEY
Book Silver Medal

*Finally they found on the dock one of those old nocturnal coupés that one sees
in Paris after nightfall, as if they were ashamed of their misery by day.*
"What a treat it is for an illustrator to be asked to visually interpret an
entire book of words like these from Guy de Maupassant. *Merci
beaucoup!*"

119

Artist: **JERRY PINKNEY**

Art Director: David Tommasino

Client: Scholastic Inc.

Size: 14 x 15

JERRY PINKNEY
Book Silver Medal

"I have long been interested in the Underground Railroad and especially the heroine, Harriet Tubman. This painting represents the triumph and survival of an enslaved people over their enslavers. One can only wonder about this woman's courage and resolve, to risk her life over and over again to secure the freedom of others."

120

Artist: **SAELIG GALLAGHER**

Art Director: Michael Farmer

Client: Harcourt Brace Jovanovich

Medium: Oil

SAELIG GALLAGHER
Book Silver Medal

"To infuse an inner life into an image, into a character and its setting—
this is what a fairy tale calls upon us to do as we work with it and
attempt to find its visual counterpoint. One of the most compelling
things about fairy tales, I find, is the way the mind receives them, the
naturalness with which we dismiss the authority of rationality and enter
the dreamscape. That we shift our awareness to recognize in them
poetic truth is perhaps equivalent to what we value most in painting:
the recognition (in physical fact) of a state of being."

121

Artist: **JOE CIARDIELLO**

Art Director: Patrick J.B. Flynn

Client: Spanfeller Press

Medium: Pen and ink

Size: 13 x 8

122

Artist: **JOE CIARDIELLO**

Art Director: Patrick J.B. Flynn

Client: Spanfeller Press

Medium: Pen and ink

Size: 13 ³/4 x 10

123

Artist: **JOHN SANDFORD**

Art Director: Marc Cheshire

Client: Arcade Publishing

Size: 18 x 24

124

Artist: **JIM BURNS**

Art Director: Jamie Warren-Youll

Client: Bantam Books

Medium: Oil on board

Size: 19 x 17

125

Artist: **JOHN SANDFORD**

Art Director: Marc Cheshire

Client: Arcade Publishing

Size: 20 x 46

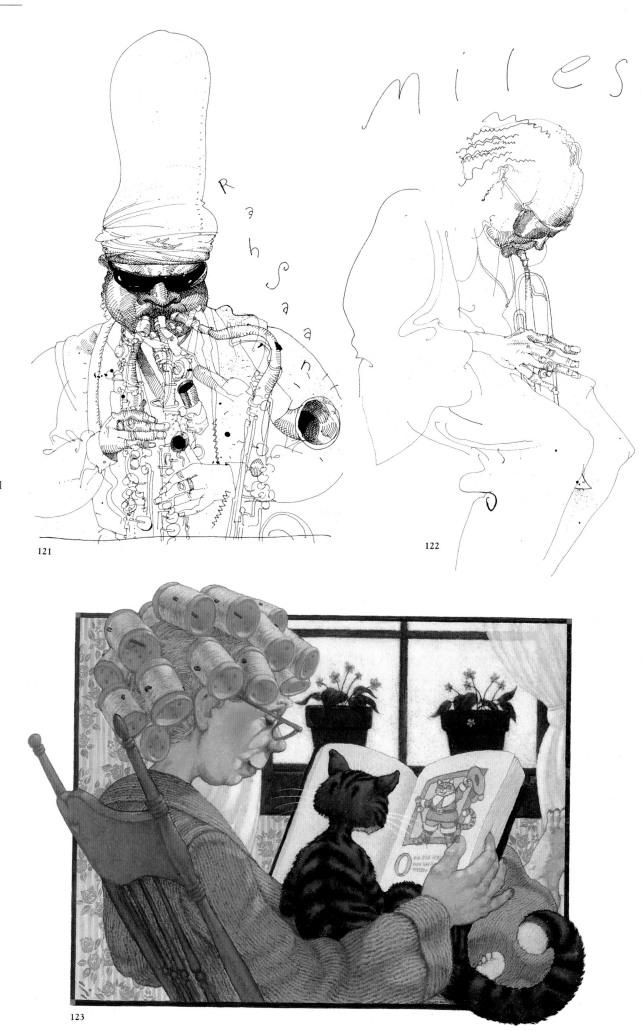

121

122

123

124

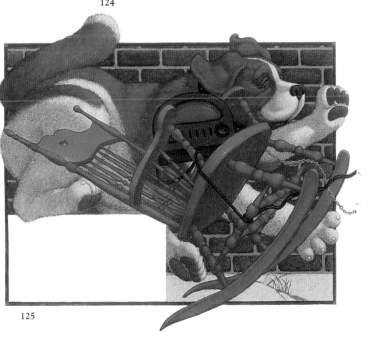

126

Artist: **GARNET HENDERSON**

Art Director: Michaela Sullivan

Client: Houghton Mifflin

Size: 6 x 6

127

Artist: **JOE CIARDIELLO**

Art Director: Patrick J.B. Flynn

Client: Spanfeller Press

Medium: Pen and ink

Size: 11 x 12 $\frac{1}{2}$

128

Artist: **STEVEN ASSEL**

Art Director: Yook Louie

Client: Bantam Books

Medium: Acrylic

Size: 37 x 51

129

Artist: **WARREN CHANG**

Medium: Oil

Size: 15 x 11

130

Artist: **STEVEN ASSEL**

Art Director: Yook Louie

Client: Bantam Books

Medium: Oil

Size: 24 x 20

126

127

128

129

130

131

Artist: **JEFF CORNELL**

Medium: Graphite

Size: 10 x 12

132

Artist: **PATRICIA ROHRBACHER**

Size: 11 1/2 x 12

133

Artist: **GARY KELLEY**

Art Directors: Tom Peterson
Louise Fili

Client: Creative Education

Medium: Pastel

Size: 18 1/2 x 23 1/2

134

Artist: **JOHN THOMPSON**

Art Director: Larissa Lawrynenko

Client: Reader's Digest General
Books

Medium: Oil

Size: 14 x 9

135

Artist: **DAVID SHANNON**

Art Director: Michael Farmer

Client: Harcourt Brace Jovanovich

Medium: Acrylic

131

132

133

134

135

136

Artist: **KAZUHIKO SANO**

Art Director: Hiroko Kodama

Client: Shincho-Sha Publishing

Medium: Acrylic

Size: 18 x 13

137

Artist: **KAZUHIKO SANO**

Art Director: Chihiro Takahashi

Client: Shincho-Sha Publishing

Medium: Acrylic

Size: 23 x 17

138

Artist: **MARK SCHULER**

Art Director: Soren Noring

Client: Reader's Digest

Medium: Watercolor

Size: 13 x 9

139

Artist: **ELAINE DUILLO**

Art Director: James Harris

Client: Ballantine Books

Medium: Acrylic

Size: 18 x 25

137

138

139

140

Artist: **DORIAN VALLEJO**

Art Director: Tom Egner

Client: Avon Books

Medium: Oil on illustration board

Size: 23 x 15 1/2

141

Artist: **DORIAN VALLEJO**

Art Director: Jamie Warren Youll

Client: Bantam Books

Medium: Oil on illustration board

Size: 24 x 15

142

Artist: **MICHAEL J. DEAS**

Art Director: Elizabeth Parisi

Medium: Oil

Size: 23 x 19 1/2

143

Artist: **JEFFREY TOMAKA**

Medium: Pastel, oil

Size: 11 x 20 3/8

141

142

143

144

Artist: **PETER DE SÈVE**

Art Director: Paul Elliot

Client: Rabbit Ears

Size: 14 x 13

145

Artist: **ELAINE DUILLO**

Art Director: Gerald Counihan

Client: Dell Publishing Company

Medium: Acrylic

Size: 17 ¹/₂ x 16 ¹/₂

146

Artist: **STEPHEN YOULL**

Art Director: Jamie Warren Youll

Client: Bantam Books

Medium: Acrylic, oil

Size: 27 x 37

147

Artist: **LISA FALKENSTERN
MILTON CHARLES**

Art Director: Milton Charles

Client: Delphinium Press

Medium: Oil

Size: 11 ¹/₂ x 8 ¹/₂

148

Artist: **STASYS
EIDRIGEVICIUS**

Client: Viking Penguin

Size: 15 x 18

144

145

146

147

148

149

Artist: **PETER SCANLAN**

Art Director: Susan Newman

Client: Macmillan Publishing
Company

Medium: Acrylic

Size: 17 x 17

150

Artist: **JOHN COLLIER**

Art Director: Alex Jay

Client: Viking Children's Books

Medium: Pastel, gouache

151

Artist: **JERRY PINKNEY**

Art Director: Atha Tehon

Client: Dial Books for Young
Readers

Size: 12 x 19 3/4

152

Artist: **LISA FALKENSTERN**

Art Director: Milton Charles

Client: Delphinium Press

Medium: Oil

Size: 11 1/2 x 9

153

Artist: **TOM CURRY**

Art Director: Kym Abrams

Client: Scott Foresman

Medium: Acrylic

Size: 14 x 11

149

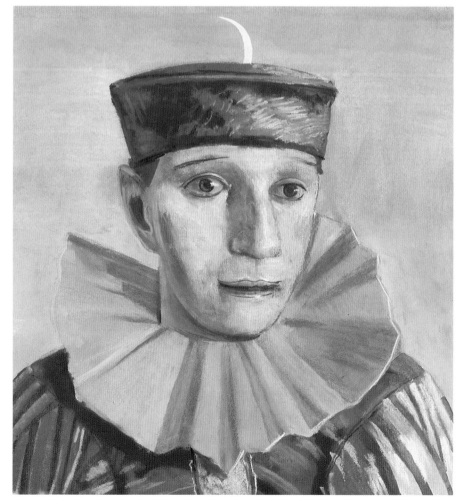

150

151

152

153

154

Artist: **DELANA BETTOLI**

Art Director: Linda Huber

Client: Silver Press/Simon & Schuster Books

Medium: Gouache

Size: 10 x 7 7/8

155

Artist: **LOIS EHLERT**

Art Director: Harriet Barton

Client: HarperCollins

Medium: Cut paper

Size: 12 1/2 x 14 3/4

156

Artist: **CHRISTOPHER MOELLER**

Art Director: George Broderick

Client: Innovation Corporation

Medium: Mixed media

Size: 25 1/2 x 15 1/2

157

Artist: **BRYAN LEISTER**

Art Director: Racquel Jaramillo

Client: Henry Holt and Co. Inc.

Size: 15 x 10

158

Artist: **ANTHONY CARNABUCI**

Art Directors: Cecilia Yung
Barbara Henessey

Client: Viking Children's Books

Medium: Oil

Size: 9 x 16

154

155

156

157

158

159

Artist: **HEIDE OBERHEIDE**

Art Director: Tom Egner

Client: Avon Books

Size: 26 x 16

160

Artist: **C. MICHAEL DUDASH**

Art Director: Gerald Counihan

Client: Delacorte Press

Medium: Oil on linen

Size: 31 x 20 1/2

161

Artist: **C. MICHAEL DUDASH**

Art Director: Gerald Counihan

Client: Dell Publishing Company

Medium: Oil on linen

Size: 27 x 18

162

Artist: **CHRISTOPHER MANSON**

Art Director: Marc Cheshire

Client: North-South Books

Size: 13 1/2 x 25 1/2

160

161

163

Artist: **RICK LOVELL**

Art Director: Tom Egner

Client: Avon Books

Size: 18 ¹/₂ x 12

164

Artist: **JEAN-FRANCOIS PODEVIN**

Art Director: Judith Murello

Client: Berkley Publishing

Size: 19 x 11 ³/₄

165

Artist: **JOHN JUDE PALENCAR**

Art Director: David Saylor

Client: HarperCollins

Medium: Watercolor, acrylic

Size: 22 x 16

166

Artist: **BARRY MOSER**

Art Director: Christine Kettner

Client: HarperCollins

Size: 9 x 19

163

164

165

166

167

Artist: **MANUEL GARCIA**

Art Director: Michael Farmer

Client: Harcourt Brace Jovanovich

Medium: Acrylic

Size: 17 x 13 1/2

168

Artist: **JOHN THOMPSON**

Art Director: Angelo Perrone

Client: Reader's Digest Condensed
Books

Medium: Acrylic

Size: 30 x 40

169

Artist: **BOB LARKIN**

Art Director: Whitney Cookman

Client: Doubleday

170

Artist: **JOEL PETER JOHNSON**

Art Directors: Bob Aulicino
Bob Scudellari

Client: Random House

Medium: Mixed media

Size: 9 x 7

168

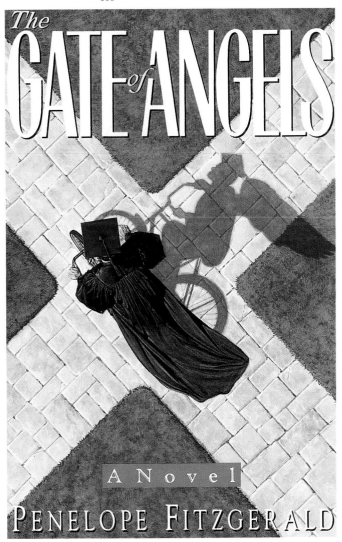

169

170

171

Artist: **PAUL MORIN**

Art Director: Michael Farmer

Client: Harcourt Brace Jovanovich

Medium: Oil

Size: 26 1/2 x 21 1/2

172

Artist: **JOHN JUDE PALENCAR**

Art Director: Judith Murello

Client: Berkley Books/Ace Books

Medium: Watercolor, acrylic

Size: 17 x 21

173

Artist: **DAVID JOHNSON**

Art Director: Larissa Lawrynenko

Client: Reader's Digest

Size: 14 x 9 1/2

174

Artist: **JIM DEAL**

Art Director: Gerald Counihan

Client: Dell Publishing Company

Medium: Acrylic

Size: 14 x 9

171

172

173

174

175

Artist: **ROBERT HYNES**

Medium: Acrylic

Size: 12 x 9

176

Artist: **MITCHELL HOOKS**

Art Director: Lorraine Paradowski

Client: Harlequin Books

Medium: Oil

Size: 19 x 14 1/2

177

Artist: **MARK RYDEN**

Art Director: Catherine
              Vandercasteele

Client: LA 411

Medium: Oil

Size: 10 1/2 x 16

178

Artist: **TED COCONIS**

Art Director: Tom Egner

Client: Avon Books

Medium: Oil on canvas

Size: 24 x 36

176

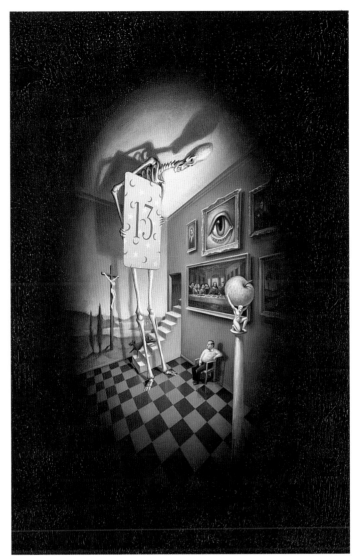

177

178

179

Artist: **MICHAEL J. DEAS**

Art Director: Barbara Leff

Medium: Oil on panel

Size: 20 x 13

180

Artist: **JIM BURNS**

Art Director: Ruth Ross

Client: Ballantine Books

Medium: Acrylic

Size: 25 x 17

181

Artist: **TOM SCIACCA**

Art Director: Jamie Warren Youll

Client: Doubleday

Medium: Acrylic

Size: 10 x 7

182

Artist: **PETER DE SEVE**

Art Director: Paul Elliot

Client: Rabbit Ears

Size: 10 1/2 x 16

180

181

182

183

Artist: **DENIS BEAUVAIS**

Art Director: Judith Murello

Client: Berkley Publishing Group

Size: 36 x 26

184

Artist: **JIM BARKLEY**

Art Director: Larissa Lawrynenko

Client: Reader's Digest General
    Books

Medium: Oil

Size: 19 x 14

185

Artist: **ROBERT CRAWFORD**

Art Director: David Bamford

Client: Berkley Publishing Group

Medium: Acrylic

Size: 16 1/2 x 10

186

Artist: **ROBERT HYNES**

Art Director: David Seager

Client: National Geographic

Medium: Acrylic

Size: 11 x 13 1/2

183

184

185

186

187

Artist: **LIANA SOMAN**

Medium: Oil on illustration board

Size: 15 1/2 x 12

188

Artist: **GARY HEAD**

Medium: Oil

Size: 13 1/2 x 17 1/2

189

Artist: **STEPHEN T. JOHNSON**

Art Director: Donna Martin

Client: Andrews and McMeel

Medium: Pastel, watercolor

Size: 21 x 16 1/4

190

Artist: **ADAM NIKLEWICZ**

Art Directors: Doris Borowsky-
Straus
Michael Accordino

Client: St. Martin's Press

Medium: Acrylic

Size: 12 x 7 1/2

187

188

189

190

191

Artist: **ROBERT McGINNIS**

Art Director: Marva Martin

Client: Bantam Books

Size: 16 x 11 1/2

192

Artist: **KEN LAAGER**

Medium: Oil

Size: 18 x 24

193

Artist: **FRED OTNES**

Art Director: Kazko Nogouchi

Client: The Greatest Illustration
Show of America

Medium: Collage

Size: 14 x 11 1/2

194

Artist: **DAVID SHANNON**

Art Directors: Gunto Alexander
Nanette Stevenson

Client: G.P. Putnam Sons

Medium: Acrylic

Size: 17 x 13

191

192

193

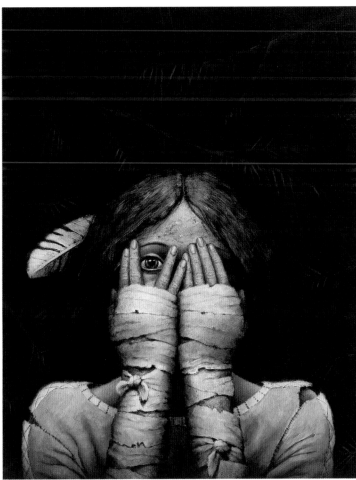

194

195

Artist: **JEAN PIERRE TARGETE**

Art Director: Diane Luger

Client: Berkley Books

Medium: Oil

Size: 25 x 17

196

Artist: **MURRAY TINKELMAN**

Medium: Pen and ink

Size: 20 x 16

197

Artist: **PHILIP SINGER**

Art Director: Jackie Merri Meyer

Client: Warner Books

Size: 8 1/2 x 7

198

Artist: **CATHERINE HUERTA**

Art Director: Al Cetta

Client: HarperCollins

Size: 19 1/2 x 18

196

197

198

199

Artist: **RICK BERRY**

Art Director: Arnie Fenner

Client: Mark V. Ziesing

Medium: Oil

Size: 29 1/2 x 19

200

Artist: **TONY O. CHAMPAGNE**

Art Directors: Trent Angers
William 'Buz' Carter

Client: Lou Ana Gardens

Size: 19 x 14 1/2

201

Artist: **TOM TAGGART**

Art Director: Tom Peyer

Client: DC Comics

Medium: 3-D, mixed media

Size: 20 1/2 x 13 1/2

202

Artist: **KIRK REINERT**

Art Director: Gene Mydlowski

Client: Harper Paperbacks

Medium: Oil

Size: 29 1/2 x 18

203

Artist: **WENDELL MINOR**

Art Director: Al Cetta

Client: HarperCollins

Medium: Watercolor, gouache

Size: 10 x 7

199

200

201

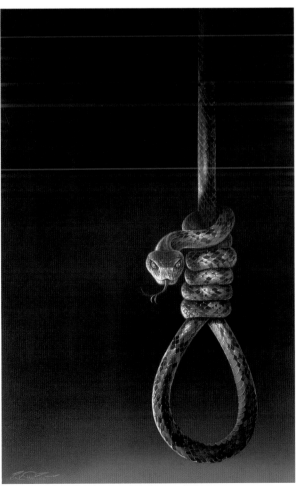

202

203

204

Artist: **KEVIN HAWKES**

Art Director: Audrey Bryant

Client: David R. Godine Publisher

Size: 13 3/4 x 11 1/4

205

Artist: **DEREK JAMES**

Art Director: Hollie A. Rubin

Client: Scholastic Inc.

Medium: Oil

Size: 17 x 10 1/2

206

Artist: **DANIEL SCHWARTZ**

Art Director: Don Owens

Client: American Jury Trial
Foundation

Size: 20 x 16

207

Artist: **ROBERT ANDREW
PARKER**

Art Director: Cecilia Yung

Client: Viking Children's Books

Medium: Etching, aquatint

Size: 8 x 6

208

Artist: **DAVID STIMSON**

Art Director: Tom Egner

Client: Avon Books

Size: 18 1/2 x 13

204

205

206

207

208

209

Artist: **KEN LAAGER**

Art Director: Yook Louie

Client: Bantam Books

Medium: Oil

Size: 24 x 16

210

Artist: **LANE SMITH**

Art Director: Molly Leach

Client: Viking Children's Books

Medium: Oil

Size: 12 1/2 x 10 1/4

211

Artist: **JOHN H. HOWARD**

Art Director: Jackie Merri Meyer

Client: Mysterious Press/
Warner Books

Size: 24 x 18

212

Artist: **KEN LAAGER**

Art Director: Yook Louie

Client: Bantam Books

Size: 18 x 24 3/4

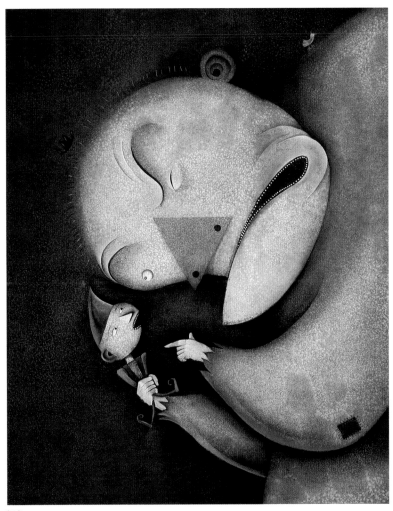

210

211

212

213

Artist: **LIANA SOMAN**

Art Director: Elizabeth Parisi

Client: Scholastic Inc.

Medium: Oil on illustration board

Size: 18 x 12

214

Artist: **MICHAEL J. DEAS**

Art Director: David Saylor

Client: HarperCollins

Size: 21 x 14

215

Artist: **DAVE CUTLER**

Art Director: Tom Mack

Client: Macmillan Publishing
Company

Medium: Acrylic

Size: 14 x 11

216

Artist: **ERIC DINYER**

Art Director: Anne Twomey

Client: Warner Books

Medium: Oil

Size: 11 x 14

217

Artist: **ERIC DINYER**

Art Director: Anne Twomey

Client: Warner Books

Medium: Oil

Size: 12 ¹/2 x 8 ³/4

213

214

215

216

217

218

Artist: **ROBERT HUNT**

Art Director: Charlotte Bralds

Client: Earth Island Institute/
Graphis

Size: 43 x 40

219

Artist: **FRED OTNES**

Art Director: Kazko Nogouchi

Client: The Greatest Illustration
Show of America

Medium: Mixed-media collage

Size: 24 x 32

220

Artist: **JOHN JUDE
PALENCAR**

Art Director: Sheila Gilbert

Client: Daw Books

Medium: Watercolor, acrylic

Size: 20 1/2 x 21

221

Artist: **PHIL PARKS**

Art Director: Ann Spinelli

Client: Putnam Publishing

Medium: Acrylic

Size: 18 x 12

218

219

220

221

222

Artist: **TOM NACHREINER**

Medium: Watercolor, gouache

Size: 23 x 31 1/2

223

Artist: **DAVID CUNNINGHAM**

Art Director: Karen Campbell

Client: Albert Whitman & Company

Medium: Gouache

Size: 6 1/2 x 6

224

Artist: **JEFF CORNELL**

Medium: Charcoal

Size: 28 x 18

225

Artist: **STEPHEN T. JOHNSON**

Art Director: Donna Martin

Client: Andrews and McMeel

Medium: Pastel, watercolor

Size: 21 x 16 1/4

226

Artist: **WILLIAM JOYCE**

Art Director: Christine Kettner

Client: HarperCollins

Size: 7 1/2 x 11

222

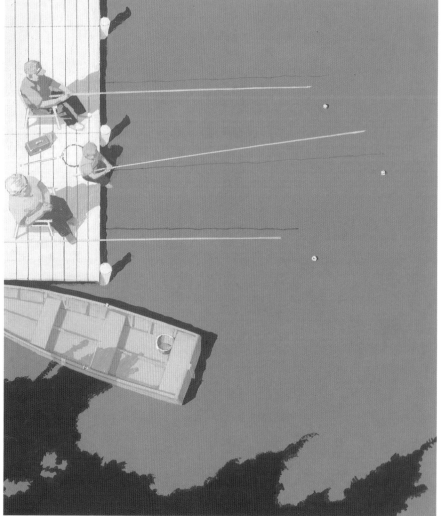

223

224

225

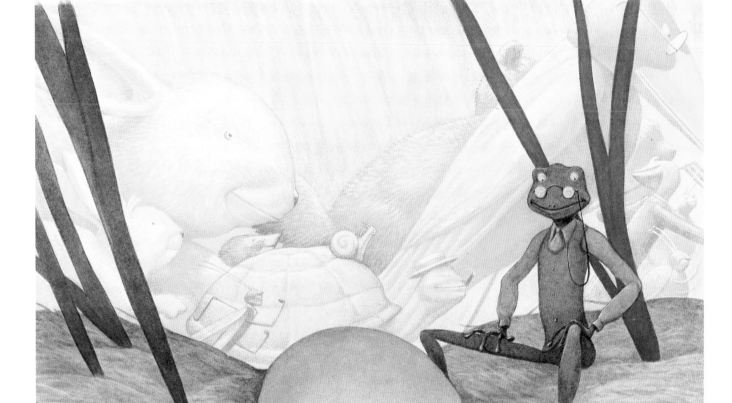

226

227

Artist: **FRED OTNES**

Medium: Mixed-media collage

Size: 21 x 22

228

Artist: **BRUCE JENSEN**

Art Director: Jamie Warren Youll

Client: Bantam Books

Medium: Acrylic/CG

Size: 14 x 11

229

Artist: **JERRY PINKNEY**

Art Director: Atha Tehon

Client: Dial Books for Young
        Readers

Size: 12 x 19 3/4

230

Artist: **JOHN COLLIER**

Art Director: Paul Buckley

Client: Penguin USA

Medium: Oil pastel

Size: 28 1/2 x 20 1/2

231

Artist: **BOB RAFEI**

Medium: Oil

Size: 36 x 24

227

228

229

230

231

232

Artist: **SHANNON STIRNWEIS**

Medium: Oil

Size: 36 x 24

233

Artist: **RICHARD SPARKS**

Art Director: Michael Baldyga

Client: Easton Press

Medium: Oil

Size: 20 x 14

234

Artist: **RICHARD SPARKS**

Art Director: Michael Baldyga

Client: Easton Press

Medium: Oil

Size: 21 x 16

235

Artist: **TOM NACHREINER**

Medium: Watercolor

Size: 22 x 29 1/2

232

233

234

235

236

Artist: **MICHAEL J. DEAS**

Art Director: Hollie A. Rubin

Client: Scholastic Inc.

Medium: Oil

Size: 16 x 11

237

Artist: **ALEX SCHAEFER**

Medium: Oil

Size: 24 x 15 1/2

238

Artist: **MARC ERICKSEN**

Art Director: James Harris

Client: Ballantine Books

Size: 40 x 35

239

Artist: **TRACI HAYMANS**

Medium: Pastel with linseed

Size: 10 x 11

240

Artist: **CATHLEEN TOELKE**

Art Director: Jackie Merri Meyer

Client: Mysterious Press/
Warner Books

Size: 9 x 6

237

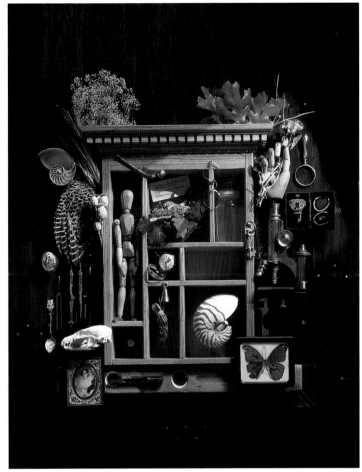

238

239

240

241

Artist: **ED LINDLOF**

Art Director: Neil Stuart

Client: Dutton Books

Medium: Pen, ink, Rotring Artist
Color

Size: 14 x 12

242

Artist: **C. BRUCE DUPREE**

Medium: Colored pencil,
watercolor

Size: 15 x 10

243

Artist: **TED COCONIS**

Medium: Oil

Size: 30 x 39

244

Artist: **PAUL BACHEM**

Art Director: Elizabeth Parisi

Client: Scholastic Inc.

Medium: Oil

Size: 32 x 22

245

Artist: **JIM BARKLEY**

Art Director: Larissa Lawrynenko

Client: Reader's Digest General
Books

Medium: Oil

Size: 14 1/2 x 19 1/2

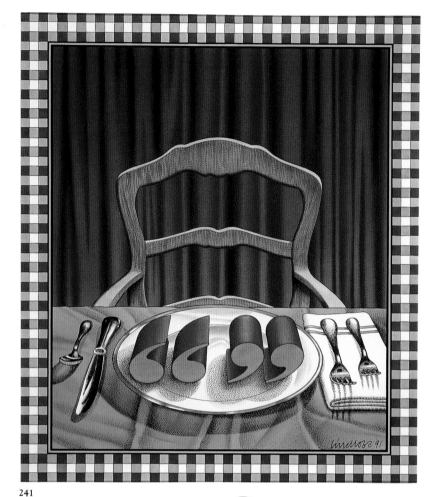

241

242

243

244

245

ADVERTISING JURY

JOHN WITT
CHAIRMAN
Creative Director/Illustrator

TINA ADAMEK
Executive Art Director
McGraw-Hill Healthcare

DAVID BLOSSOM
Illustrator

JOHN COLLIER
Illustrator

ALAN E. COBER
Illustrator

MICHAEL GARLAND
Illustrator

ENID V. HATTON
Illustrator

BURT SILVERMAN
Illustrator/Painter

ATHA TEHON
Associate Publisher/Art Director
Dial Books for Young Readers

ADVERTISING

AWARD WINNERS

KINUKO Y. CRAFT
Gold Medal

MICHAEL J. DEAS
Gold Medal

WIKTOR SADOWSKI
Gold Medal

WILLIAM LOW
Silver Medal

MARK SUMMERS
Silver Medal

KINUKO Y. CRAFT
Advertising Gold Medal

"The best moment in the creation of one of my illustrations is whe[...]
can begin to see the image forming in the board, almost as if it we[...]
empty box, before I have ever touched the surface. At that mome[...]
is most full of hope and dreams, and all things are possible."

247

Artist: **MICHAEL J. DEAS**

Art Director: Jim Cotton

Agency: Jim Cotton
    Communications

Client: Ghurka Luggage

Medium: Oil on panel

Size: 16 x 24

MICHAEL J. DEAS
Advertising Gold Medal

"This painting, done on panel for Ghurka Luggage, was a complete campaign image used in many ways, shapes, and sizes from stamps to posters. The objective in this advertisement was to give the product a classic, timeless look—it could be 1933 or 1993."

248

Artist: **WIKTOR SADOWSKI**

Art Director: Wiktor Sadowski

Client: Polish Film

Medium: Oil

Size: 23 x 16

Advertising Gold Medal

This poster for the movie by Peter Greenaway, *The Draughtsman's Contract*, was assigned by the distributor of this movie in Sadowski's native Poland. The atmosphere is full of insinuation; it is magical and mysterious and allows one to create a visual image, free from literal translation.

Artist: **WILLIAM LOW**

Art Director: Drennan Lindsay

Client: Eddie Bauer

Size: 20 x 20

WILLIAM LOW
Advertising Silver Medal

" 'Orcas Island Ferry' is my second Eddie Bauer catalog cover illustration and my first assignment since moving from New York where I have always lived. Now I'm living and painting in a suburban, semi-rural sprawl. Because my paintings are about light, many people assume that I have a sun-drenched studio. In reality, it is in the small damp basement of my house without sunlight but full of spiders and fluorescent lights. To overcome these problems, I use a lot of imagination, some photographic reference and inspiration from many artists: Fairfield Porter, Isaak Levitan, Richard Diebenkorn, Claude Monet, and Edward Hopper. I understand from letters responding to the Eddie Bauer cover that Orcas Island *is* a beautiful place and that I've captured the feeling of these islands. It sounds like it could make for a lovely vacation. Maybe one day I can experience this feeling for *myself*."

Artist: **MARK SUMMERS**

Art Director: Michael Fountain

Agency: Ice Communications, Inc.

Client: Remington Steel

Medium: Scratchboard, watercolor

Size: 9 x 8

MARK SUMMERS
Advertising Silver Medal

This ad for Remington Steel, makers of quality shotgun shells, was the first piece Mark did in his new home in Ontario. Rumor in the community had it that he was an artist...and that the neighbors weren't quite sure what to expect. Mark saw a big guy jogging past one day, stopped him, and asked if he wouldn't mind modeling for an advertisement. It turns out the guy was a cop and once he saw the layout, he got enthused. Word spread that the new artist was not a "weirdo type" and soon he was accepted in the neighborhood.

251

Artist: **ROBERT HUNT**

Art Director: Chuck Stern

Agency: Foote Cone & Belding

Client: Baykeepers

Medium: Oil

Size: 33 x 24

252

Artist: **PATRICK D. MILBOURN**

Medium: Oil

Size: 30 x 15

253

Artist: **CHRIS HOPKINS**

Art Director: Bill Sweeney

Client: Silver Creek Farms

Medium: Oil

Size: 14 x 22

251

252

253

254

Artist: **BRALDT BRALDS**

Art Director: Arnie Arlow

Agency: TBWA

Client: Carillon Imports

Medium: Oil

Size: 24 x 20

255

Artist: **BRALDT BRALDS**

Art Director: Arnie Arlow

Agency: TBWA

Client: Carillon Imports

Medium: Oil

Size: 24 x 20

256

Artist: **RICH BOWMAN**

Art Director: George Kaufman

Agency: Kuhn & Wittenborn

Client: Baskin Robbins

Medium: Oil

Size: 20 1/2 x 10

257

Artist: **MARY GRANDPRÉ**

Art Director: David Bartels

Agency: Bartels Associates

Client: GDS

Medium: Pastel

Size: 13 x 24 1/2

254

255

256

257

258

Artist: **KATHERINE
LANDIKUSIC**

Art Director: Martha Swords

Client: Prince of Whales Polo Cup

Medium: Pastel

Size: 36 x 22

259

Artist: **FRANCES JETTER**

Art Director: Taras Wayner

Agency: Mad Dogs & Englishmen

Client: Audubon

Size: 18 x 11

260

Artist: **JOHN JUDE
PALENCAR**

Art Director: Diane Stegmeier

Client: Steelcase

Medium: Watercolor, acrylic

Size: 16 1/2 x 14

261

Artist: **CHARLES SANTORE**

Art Director: Bernie Hogya

Agency: Bozell, Inc.

Client: Merrill Lynch

Medium: Watercolor

Size: 11 x 8

262

Artist: **CRAIG FRAZIER**

Art Director: Craig Frazier

Client: Mill Valley Film Festival

Medium: Cut paper

Size: 14 1/2 x 11

258

259

260

261

262

263

Artist: **BERNIE FUCHS**

Art Director: Drennan Lindsay

Client: Eddie Bauer

Medium: Oil

Size: 26 x 26

264

Artist: **JOEL PETER JOHNSON**

Art Director: Suzanne Adrian

Client: Koch International Classics

Size: 6 x 6

265

Artist: **WILLIAM LOW**

Art Director: Peter Schaefer

Client: The New York Times

Size: 10 x 15 1/2

266

Artist: **JOYCE PATTI**

Art Director: Becky Connell-
    Swanson

Agency: DMB & B

Client: LaSalle Banks

Medium: Oil

Size: 17 x 11

267

Artist: **JOYCE PATTI**

Art Director: Becky Connell-
    Swanson

Agency: DMB & B

Client: LaSalle Banks

Medium: Oil

Size: 17 x 11

263

264

265

266

267

268

Artist: **CARY AUSTIN**

Art Director: Randy Smith

Agency: Randall Smith Associates

Client: Pioneer Theatre Company

Medium: Acrylic

Size: 18 x 15 3/4

269

Artist: **FRANCIS LIVINGSTON**

Art Director: Chris Knight

Agency: Macy's

Client: Macy's

Size: 24 x 24

270

Artist: **CATHLEEN TOELKE**

Art Director: Shuzo Hirata

Agency: Hakuhodo Inc.

Client: Cecilene

Medium: Gouache

Size: 19 x 14

271

Artist: **PAUL ROGERS**

Art Director: Robert Upisandi

Agency: Saatchi & Saatchi

Client: Toyota

Medium: Acrylic

Size: 30 x 20

272

Artist: **F. XAVIER PAVY**

Art Director: Frank Olinsky

Client: Sire/Reprise Records

Medium: Oil

Size: 24 x 24

268

269

270

271

272

273

Artist: **LAURA PHILLIPS**

Art Director: Claude Prettyman

Client: Red Robin Restaurants

Medium: Acrylic, airbrush

Size: 24 x 22

274

Artist: **MARY JO PHALEN**

Art Director: Mary Jo Phalen

Client: San Diego Zoo Wild
Animal Park

Medium: Mixed media

Size: 28 x 36

275

Artist: **BART FORBES**

Art Director: Rich Burk

Client: The Fred Meyer Challenge

Medium: Oil on canvas

Size: 18 1/2 x 27 1/2

276

Artist: **TIM LEWIS**

277

Artist: **BERNIE FUCHS**

Art Director: Helene Sigman

Client: Ameritech

Medium: Oil

Size: 35 x 24

273

274

275

276

277

278

Artist: **DUGALD STERMER**

Art Director: Melanie Doherty

Client: DFS Group, Ltd.

Medium: Pencil, watercolor on Arches

Size: 20 x 12

279

Artist: **DUGALD STERMER**

Art Director: Greg McGough

Agency: SlaughterHanson Advertising

Client: Southern Natural Gas

Medium: Pencil, watercolor on Arches

280

Artist: **TRISTAN A. ELWELL**

Art Director: Dick Calderhead

Agency: Calderhead & Phin

Client: Willis Corroon

Medium: Oil on gessoed paper

Size: 12 x 9

281

Artist: **WARREN LINN**

Art Director: Stephen Byram

Client: JMT Productions

Medium: Acrylic, collage on plywood

Size: 36 x 24

282

Artist: **MIKE REAGAN**

Art Director: Albert Chiang

Client: Islands Magazine

Medium: Watercolor, ink

Size: 16 x 21

278

279

280

281

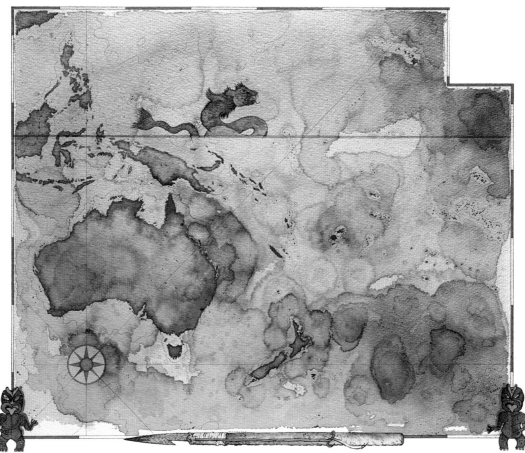

282

283

Artist: **JERRY LOFARO**

Art Director: Woody Litwhiler

Agency: Bozell, Inc.

Client: Minolta

Medium: Acrylic

Size: 26 x 20

284

Artist: **GERALDINE CONEY**

Medium: Paper sculpture

Size: 18 x 18

285

Artist: **PAUL MICICH**

Art Director: Randy Messer

Client: Perfection Learning

Medium: Alkyd

Size: 25 x 20

286

Artist: **MILAN KECMAN**

Art Director: Sue Monahan

Agency: Glazen Advertising

Client: National City Bank

Medium: Scratchboard

Size: 9 x 6

287

Artist: **MARVIN MATTELSON**

Art Director: June Robinson

Agency: McCaffrey & McCall

Client: A & E

Medium: Oil

Size: 10 x 8

283

284

285

286

287

288

Artist: **WILLIAM C. BURGARD**

Art Director: Susan Pollay

Client: Ann Arbor Summer
Festival

Medium: Pastel, collage

Size: 45 x 30

289

Artist: **CAROLYN RIE**

Art Director: Matthew Schille

Agency: Hammond-Farrell, Inc.

Client: Integrated Network
Corporation

Medium: Tempra, gouache

Size: 12 x 14

290

Artist: **STASYS
EIDRIGEVICIUS**

Art Director: Laurie Churchman

Agency: Hewson, Berlin

Client: Commerical Risk Partners

Medium: Masks, cardboard, pastels,
guache

291

Artist: **JOHN BURGOYNE**

Art Director: Rudy Banny

Agency: Grant Jacoby

Client: Wilson Sporting Goods

Size: 35 x 18 1/2

292

Artist: **NATSUMI KAWAKAMI**

Medium: Oil

Size: 24 x 12

288

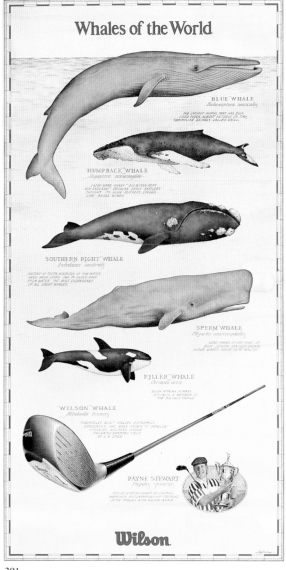

289

290

291

292

293

Artist: **ALEX MURAWSKI**

Art Director: David Bartels

Agency: Bartels Associates

Client: Gator Lager

Medium: Ink, acrylic

Size: 12 x 13

294

Artists: **GRIESBACH/ MARTUCCI**

Art Director: Doug Klein

Agency: Rapp-Collins Marcoa

Client: Rapp-Collins Marcoa

Medium: Oil on masonite

Size: 15 x 12

295

Artist: **MARVIN MATTELSON**

Art Director: Geoff Hayes

Agency: TBWA

Client: HIP

Medium: Oil

Size: 11 x 17

296

Artist: **PETER SIU**

Art Director: Gary Larsen

Agency: Larsen Colby

Medium: Oil, pen, ink on paper

Size: 7 1/2 x 6

297

Artist: **JAMES McMULLAN**

Art Director: Jim Russek

Agency: Russek Advertising

Client: Lincoln Center Theater

Medium: Watercolor

Size: 10 1/2 x 5 1/2

293

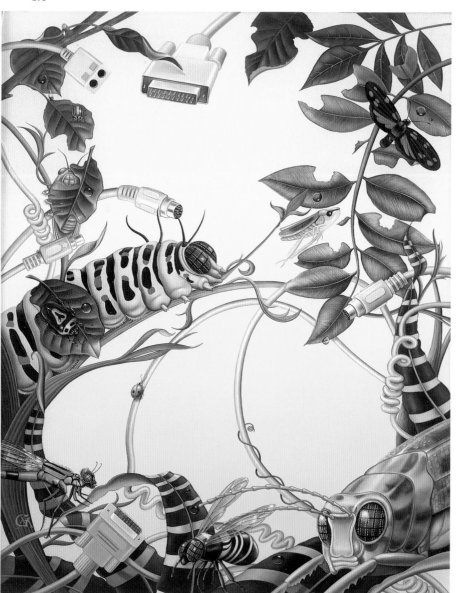

294

295

296

297

298

Artist: **TIM JESSELL**

Art Director: John Norman

Client: Nike

Medium: Pastel, mixed media

Size: 26 x 18

299

Artist: **SCOTT SWALES**

Medium: Pastel, acrylics

Size: 10 x 8 1/2

300

Artist: **PAUL DAVIS**

Art Director: Eric Baker

Client: The Body Shop

Medium: Acrylic on board

Size: 17 x 11 1/2

301

Artist: **ROBERT HUNT**

Art Directors: Henry Lehn
              Tony Seiniger

Agency: Seiniger Advertising

Client: Amblin Entertainment

Medium: Oil

Size: 38 x 24

302

Artist: **DANIEL SCHWARTZ**

Art Director: Daniel Schwartz

Client: Mobil Corporation

Medium: Oil

Size: 18 1/2 x 15

298

299

300

301

302

303

Artist: **LAURA PHILLIPS**

Art Director: Gary Larsen

Agency: Larsen Colby

Client: Austin Computer Systems

Medium: Acrylic, airbrush

Size: 12 x 14 1/2

304

Artist: **J.W. STEWART**

Client: PolyGram/Island Records

Medium: Mixed media

Size: 12 3/4 x 15 1/2

305

Artist: **BART FORBES**

Client: Dallas Arts Jazz '92

Medium: Oil

Size: 14 x 38

306

Artist: **PAUL DAVIS**

Art Director: Janice Brunell

Agency: Russek Advertising

Client: Big Apple Circus

Size: 19 1/2 x 14 1/2

307

Artist: **PAUL DAVIS**

Art Director: Janice Brunell

Agency: Russek Advertising

Client: Big Apple Circus

Size: 20 x 15

303

304

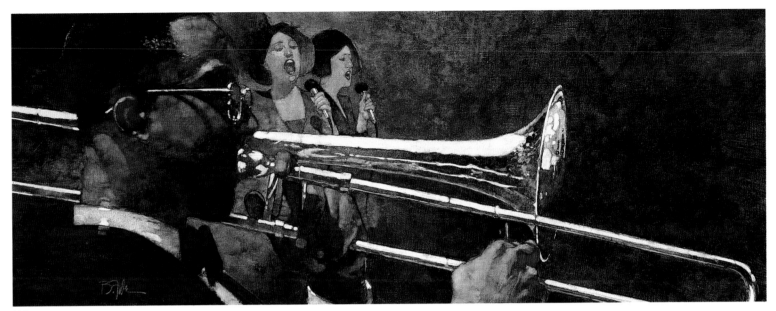

305

306

307

308

Artist: **JERRY LOFARO**

Art Director: Woody Litwhiler

Agency: Bozell, Inc.

Client: Minolta

Medium: Acrylic

Size: 26 x 20

309

Artist: **JERRY LOFARO**

Art Director: Woody Litwhiler

Agency: Bozell, Inc.

Client: Minolta

Medium: Acrylic

Size: 29 1/2 x 24 1/2

310

Artist: **ROBERT G. STEELE**

Art Director: Richard Mantel

Client: New York Magazine

Medium: Watercolor

Size: 15 1/2 x 12

311

Artist: **MARK A. FREDRICKSON**

Art Director: John Vitro

Agency: Franklin Stoorza

Client: Thermoscan

Medium: Acrylic

Size: 14 x 23

308

309

310

311

312

Artist: **FRED HILLIARD**

Art Director: Clay Turner

Agency: Ackerman McQueen

Client: Wiltel

Medium: Pen, ink, gouache

Size: 10 x 10

313

Artist: **MARK RYDEN**

Art Director: Melanie Penny

Client: Private Music

Medium: Oil

Size: 15 1/2 x 15 1/2

314

Artist: **BERNIE FUCHS**

Art Director: Karen Lothan

Agency: Hal Riney & Partners

Client: Nuveen

Medium: Oil on canvas

Size: 24 x 36

315

Artist: **JOEL NAKAMURA**

Art Directors: Nancy Donald
David Coleman

Client: Sony Music

Medium: Mixed media

Size: 27 x 13

316

Artist: **REGAN DUNNICK**

Art Director: Don Sibley

Client: Ameritrust

Medium: Pastel, oil

Size: 11 x 7 1/2

312

313

314

315

316

317

Artist: **MARK RYDEN**

Art Directors: Nancy Donald
Mark Ryden

Client: Sony Music

Medium: Oil

Size: 20 1/2 x 20 1/2

318

Artist: **PAUL DAVIS**

Art Directors: Paul Davis
Jim Russek

Agency: Russek Advertising

Client: WNCN

Medium: Acrylic on board

Size: 3 1/2 x 28

319

Artist: **GREGORY MANCHESS**

Art Directors: Gregory Manchess
Stan Thomas

Client: Homewares, Inc.

Medium: Oil

Size: 21 x 25 1/2

320

Artist: **VIVIENNE FLESHER**

Client: New York Magazine

Medium: Pastel

Size: 18 x 14

321

Artist: **CATHLEEN TOELKE**

Art Director: Carol Chen

Client: Sony Music

Medium: Gouache

Size: 9 1/2 x 6 1/2

317

318

319

320

321

322

Artist: **SKIP LIEPKE**

Art Director: Harry Kramp

Agency: J. Walter Thompson/
PPGH

Client: Heineken, Netherlands

Medium: Oil

Size: 31 1/2 x 24

323

Artist: **MARK ENGLISH**

Art Director: Jim Plumeri

Client: Bantam Books, Doubleday
Dell, Audio Publishing

Size: 21 1/2 x 13

324

Artist: **KAZUHIKO SANO**

Art Directors: Charles Davis
John Grimaldi

Agency: Davis & Grimaldi

Client: Saul Zaente Company

Medium: Acrylic

Size: 35 x 22 1/2

325

Artist: **CAROL WALD**

Art Director: Susan Russo

Client: Dennos Museum Center

Medium: Oil

Size: 72 x 216

322

323

324

325

326

Artist: **JOHN PIAMPIANO**

Medium: Acrylic

Size: 9 1/2 x 9 1/4

327

Artist: **TERRY RAVANELLI**

Art Director: Grady Phelan

Client: H.J. Heinz

Medium: Ink, watercolor

Size: 13 x 13

328

Artist: **PAUL DAVIS**

Art Director: Fran Michelman

Client: Mobil Mystery!

Medium: Acrylic on board

Size: 16 1/2 x 11

329

Artist: **RUSS WILSON**

Art Director: Russ Wilson

Client: Aslan House

Medium: Pastel

Size: 20 x 13

330

Artist: **DORI SPECTOR**

Medium: Oil

Size: 25 x 29

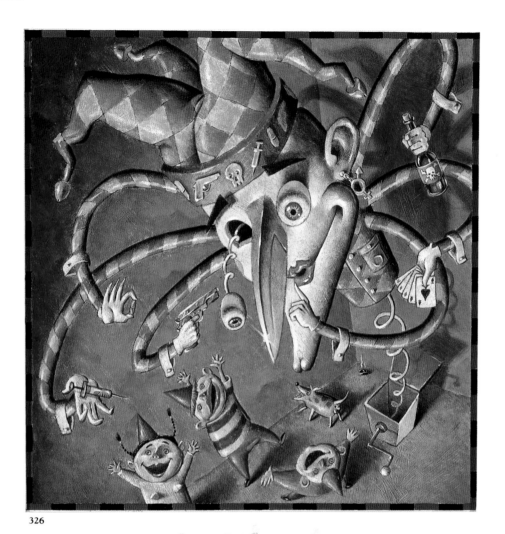

326

327

328

329

330

331

Artist: **BRALDT BRALDS**

Art Director: Jack Frakes

Agency: Ross Roy Advertising

Client: Alfa Romeo

Medium: Oil on masonite

Size: 12 x 10

332

Artist: **CORBERT GAUTHIER**

Art Director: Brent Boyd

Agency: CMF & Z

Client: Pella Windows

Medium: Oil

Size: 19 x 13

333

Artist: **ALEX MURAWSKI**

Art Director: Bruce Campbell

Agency: KSK

Client: V.M. Systems

Medium: Ink, acrylic

Size: 9 x 6

334

Artist: **JOHN THOMPSON**

Size: 8 1/2 x 11 1/2

331

332

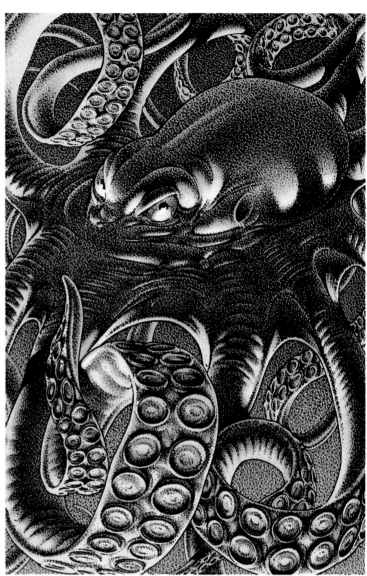

333

334

335

Artist: **JOEL SPECTOR**

Art Director: Tom McManus

Agency: TBWA

Client: Absolut Vodka

Medium: Pastel

Size: 16 x 21

336

Artist: **GERRY GERSTEN**

Art Director: Gerry Steijn

Client: Intermediair

Size: 17 x 14

337

Artist: **WIKTOR SADOWSKI**

Art Director: Wiktor Sadowski

Client: Polish Film

Medium: Oil

Size: 15 x 21

338

Artist: **RAFAL OLBINSKI**

Art Director: Alane Gehagen

Agency: Ziff Marketing

Client: New York City Opera

Medium: Acrylic on canvas

Size: 20 1/2 x 14 1/2

339

Artist: **C. MICHAEL DUDASH**

Art Director: Robin Bray

Client: Time-Life Music

Medium: Oil on gessoed gator foam

Size: 18 x 14

335

336

337

338

339

340

Artist: **ETIENNE DELESSERT**

Art Director: Steven Doyle

Agency: Drenttel-Doyle

Client: World Financial Center, NY

Medium: Watercolor

Size: 11 x 8

341

Artist: **ETIENNE DELESSERT**

Art Director: Rita Marshall

Client: Creative Education

Medium: Watercolor

Size: 11 1/2 x 8

342

Artist: **ELWOOD H. SMITH**

Art Director: Steve Curran

Client: Gametek

Medium: Watercolor, india ink

Size: 10 x 8

343

Artist: **ADAM MATHEWS**

Art Directors: Scott Fixari
Kurt Hill

Client: Responsible Dog Owners Assoc.

Medium: Acrylic

Size: 15 x 12

344

Artist: **PAUL MICICH**

Art Director: Randy Messer

Client: Perfection Learning

Medium: Alkyd, photo silkscreen

Size: 31 x 24

340

341

342

343

344

345

Artist: **VICTOR LEE**

Medium: Acrylic

Size: 14 x 11

346

Artist: **DANIEL MARK DUFFY**

Size: 30 x 46

347

Artist: **GLENN HARRINGTON**

Art Director: Glenn Harrington

Client: Artefact

Size: 9 x 7

348

Artist: **ERNEST NORCIA**

Art Director: Robin Bray

Client: Time-Life Music

Medium: Oil paint on cotton board

Size: 17 x 12 1/2

349

Artist: **LINDA DEVITO SOLTIS**

Art Director: Linda DeVito Soltis

Client: The Stephen Lawrence Company

Medium: Oil on canvas

Size: 18 x 23

345

346

347

348

349

350

Artist: **DAVID LESH**

Art Director: Jeff Larson

Client: Boeinno Assoc.

Medium: Mixed media

Size: 7 1/2 x 7

351

Artist: **SALLY WERN COMPORT**

Art Director: Dan Hooven

Agency: White, Good & Co.

Client: Mechanicsburgh Rehab System

Medium: Mixed media

Size: 14 x 16

352

Artist: **KAREN CHANDLER**

Medium: Oil

Size: 26 1/2 x 39 1/2

353

Artist: **RON FINGER**

Art Director: Carol Poulson

Client: Travellers Express

Medium: Gouache, pastel

Size: 22 x 16

354

Artist: **RAFAL OLBINSKI**

Art Director: Alane Gehagen

Agency: Ziff Marketing

Client: New York City Opera

Medium: Acrylic on canvas

Size: 20 x 30

350

351

352

353

354

355

Artist: **TIM O'BRIEN**

Medium: Oil on gessoed panel

Size: 27 ¹/₂ X 17 ¹/₂

356

Artist: **RON FINGER**

Art Director: Mike Fazande

Agency: Fallon McElligott

Client: Aveda

Medium: Watercolor

Size: 18 ¹/₂ x 13

357

Artist: **CAROLINE MICHAUD**

Art Directors: Sharon Jacobs
Carla Miller

Client: International Jugglers
Association

Medium: Pastel

Size: 38 x 24

358

Artist: **WILLIAM MATTHEWS**

Art Director: Steven Whatley

Client: Warner Western Records

Medium: Watercolor on handmade
paper

Size: 24 x 19

359

Artist: **WILLIAM MATTHEWS**

Art Director: Steven Whatley

Client: Warner Western Records

Medium: Watercolor on handmade
paper

Size: 23 x 19

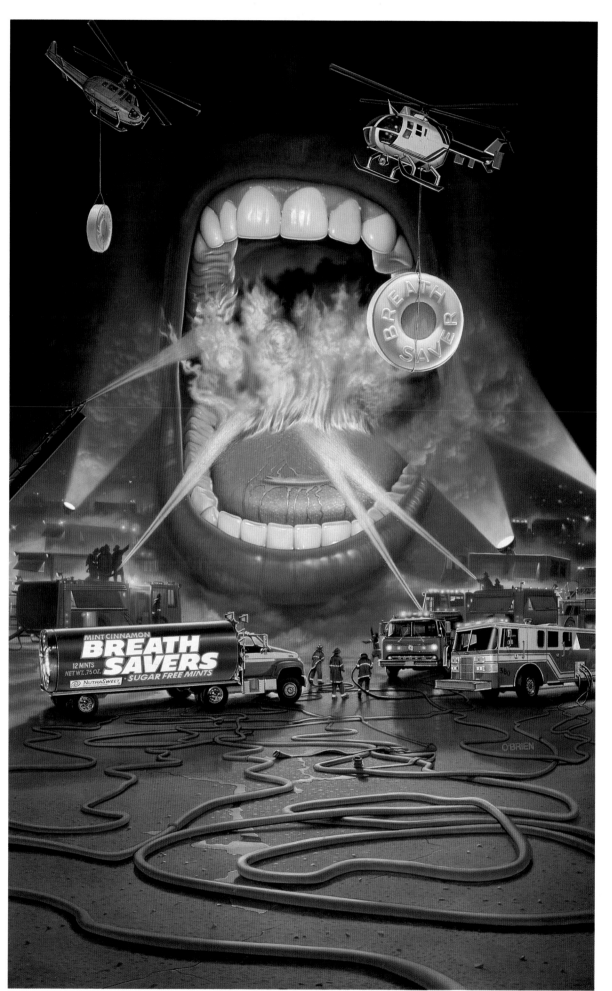

356

357

358

359

360

Artist: **MAURICE LEWIS**

Art Director: Hunter George

Agency: Johnston/George & Breslau

Client: Sterling Electronics

Medium: Oil

Size: 22 x 27

361

Artist: **PAUL SCHMID**

Art Director: Judy Dolim-Shafer

Agency: Nordstrom

Client: Nordstrom

Size: 9 1/2 x 9 1/2

362

Artist: **MIKE SCANLAN**

Art Director: Mike Scanlan

Agency: CS & A

Client: CS & A

Medium: Acrylic, colored pencil

Size: 7 x 6

363

Artist: **FRANCIS LIVINGSTON**

Agency: Corporate Graphics

Client: St. John's Hospital

Size: 11 x 8

364

Artist: **RICHARD SPARKS**

Medium: Oil on linen

Size: 30 x 40

360

361

362

363

364

365

Artist: **WIKTOR SADOWSKI**

Art Director: Alane Gehagen

Agency: Ziff Marketing

Client: National Actors Theatre

Medium: Oil

Size: 29 x 25

366

Artist: **CURTIS PARKER**

Art Director: Brad Ghormley

Client: Childsplay Theater

Size: 17 x 17

367

Artist: **JAMES McMULLAN**

Art Director: James McMullan

Client: Michael Di Capua Books/
        HarperCollins

Medium: Watercolor

Size: 9 1/4 x 8

368

Artist: **STEFANO VITALE**

Client: Pantheon/Random House

Size: 12 x 9

369

Artist: **GREGORY MANCHESS**

Art Directors: Gregory Manchess
           Stan Thomas

Client: Homewares, Inc.

Medium: Oil

Size: 18 x 30

365

366

367

368

369

370

Artist: **LELAND KLANDERMAN**

Art Director: Steve Olson

Agency: Ryan Co.

Client: Home Savings of America

371

Artist: **JOSH GOSFIELD**

Art Director: Kim Champagne

Client: Capricorn Records

Size: 50 x 34 x 9

372

Artist: **RON FINGER**

Art Director: Sally Wagner

Agency: Martin Williams Advertising

Client: Minnesota Orchestra

Medium: Acrylic

Size: 14 x 9

373

Artist: **RICHARD SPARKS**

Medium: Watercolor

Size: 30 x 22 ¹/₂

374

Artist: **BILL MAYER**

Art Director: Shirley Fee

Size: 8 ¹/₂ x 18

370

371

372

373

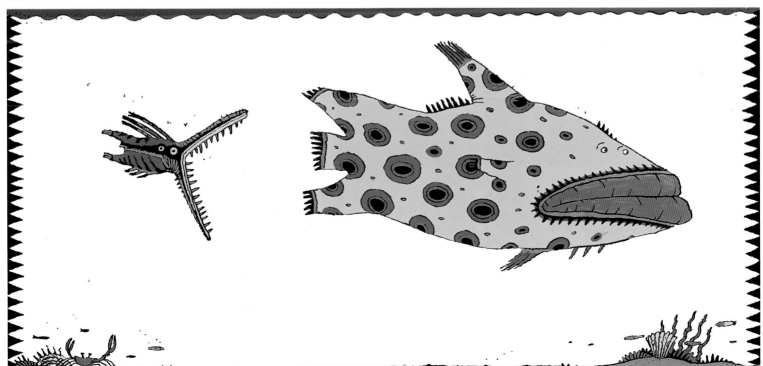

374

375

Artist: **MICHAEL GARLAND**

Art Directors: Larry Rosler
Tim Gillner

Client: Boyds Mills Press

Medium: Oil

Size: 14 x 11

376

Artist: **ELIZABETH TRAYNOR**

Art Director: Stephen Jones

Agency: Tucker Wayne Luckie
Company

Client: Reynolds Metals Company

Medium: Handcolored scratchboard

Size: 7 x 9

377

Artist: **CHERYL COOPER**

Medium: Oil

Size: 48 x 36

378

Artist: **ETIENNE DELESSERT**

Art Director: Rita Marshall

Client: Centre Design Uqam,
Canada

Medium: Watercolor

Size: 4 ³/4 x 6

375

376

377

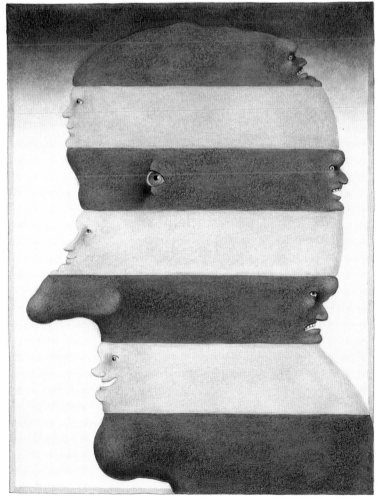

378

379

Artist: **ROBERT GIUSTI**

Art Director: Joann Tansman

Agency: BBD&O

Client: General Electric

Medium: Acrylic on canvas

Size: 14 x 14

380

Artist: **MIKE REAGAN**

Art Director: Larry Bennet

Agency: McKinney & Silver

Client: Bahamas Ministry of
Tourism

Medium: Watercolor, ink

381

Artist: **DOUG STRUTHERS**

Art Director: Ted Whitby

Agency: KPR

Client: Syntex

Medium: Computer

Size: 19 x 15 1/2

382

Artist: **VIVIENNE FLESHER**

Art Director: Vicki Morgan

Client: Rabbit Ears

Medium: Pastel

Size: 16 x 22

379

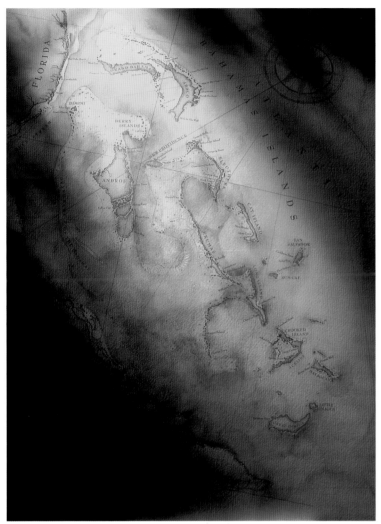

380

381

382

383

Artist: **MIKE BENNY**

Art Director: Bob Beyn

Agency: Seraphein Beyn

Client: Shanley's

Size: 17 x 18

384

Artist: **LIN H. SHEN**

Medium: Oil

Size: 13 x 15

385

Artist: **JAMES McMULLAN**

Agency: Russek Advertising

Client: Lincoln Center Theater

Size: 10 x 5

386

Artist: **PAUL MICICH**

Art Director: Randy Messer

Client: Perfection Learning

Size: 34 x 26

387

Artist: **ROGER DE MUTH**

Size: 5 ¹/2 x 8

383

384

385

386

387

INSTITUTIONAL JURY

DENNIS LYALL
CHAIRMAN
Illustrator

DAVID BARTELS
President, Bartels & Company

NICK DI DIO
Art Director
Golf Digest

H. TOM HALL
Illustrator

ROBERT HUNT
Illustrator

CHARLES KADIN
Director, Graphic Art,
Harlequin Books

HIRO KIMURA
Illustrator

ELWOOD H. SMITH
Illustrator

JOSEPH STELMACH
Senior Director
Art & Design, BMG Classics

INSTITUTIONAL

AWARD WINNERS

TRAIAN FILIP
Silver Medal

ALBERT LORENZ
Silver Medal

EDWARD SOREL
Silver Medal

HERBERT TAUSS
Silver Medal

388

Artist: **TRAIAN ALEXANDRU FILIP**

Medium: Oil, mixed media on carhood

Size: 43 x 54

TRAIAN FILIP
Institutional Silver Medal

Born in Romania, Filip holds an MFA from Grigorescu Institute of Fine Arts in Bucharest. He has lived in the U.S. since 1989, pursuing his career as a painter, etcher, and graphic artist working in a diversity of media. The award winning work "From Door to Door," was painted on a car hood. Says Filip, "Art is magic and has its own life. Sometimes when I'm working it seems like a painting is creating itself without me. I can't explain what I'm doing until I'm finished. Then I see things I wasn't conscious of before and I understand myself better, because painting comes from the deepest part of your soul."

389

Artist: **ALBERT LORENZ**

Medium: Pen, ink with watercolor

Size: 21 x 37

ALBERT LORENZ
Institutional Silver Medal

Albert Lorenz holds degrees in Architecture from Pratt Institute and Columbia University and is a Ph.D. Candidate in Anthropology at Princeton University. He has illustrated for architects, publishers, ad agencies, and editorial venues since 1969 and has authored and illustrated a number of instructional volumes about drawing and architectural illustration. His work has been included in professional exhibitions and journals including the Art Directors Show, the Society of Illustrators Exhibitions and Annuals, and *Pictorial Maps* by Nigel Holmes.

EDWARD SOREL
Institutional Silver Medal

"This appeared on a poster for an exhibition of children's book art. Dorothy and her friends from Oz are exiting at 63rd Street because that's where the exhibit was held. Illustrating posters is quite different from illustrating children's books—with posters you never get semi-annual statements informing you how much money you still owe from your advance."

tist: **EDWARD SOREL**
t Director: Marcus Ratliff
ient: Society of Illustrators
edium: Pen, ink, watercolor
ze: 10 1/2 x 16

391

Artist: **HERBERT TAUSS**

Art Director: Peter Fiore

Client: Society of Illustrators

Medium: Oil

Size: 36 x 26

HERBERT TAUSS
Institutional Silver Medal

Growing weary of posing, she stepped from the platform, holding close her robe. Approaching his easel she saw with horror how he had maligned her. She struck him—not once but over and over again, until the stretchers could no longer support the canvas. He fell to the floor. But then her hands, ever so slowly, rose to her lips in recognition. The sight of him froze her still. The paint had darkened his hair and he wore an expression of a time forgotten. Of a time long gone. She went to him and cradled him in her arms. And being the bastard that he was, he could only think, "Sargent was right. 'A portrait is a picture in which there is just a tiny little something not quite right about the mouth.' "

392

Artist: **GEORGE ANGELINI**

Art Director: Jeff Palmer

Client: American Showcase

Medium: Oil

Size: 34 x 24

393

Artist: **GEORGE Y. ABE**

Art Director: Monte Dorman

Client: KCI

Medium: Acrylic

Size: 11 x 14

394

Artist: **MIKE BENNY**

Client: ASPCA

Medium: Acrylic

Size: 12 x 9

395

Artist: **ROBERT M. CUNNINGHAM**

Client: Lustrare

Medium: Acrylic on paper

Size: 18 x 27

392

393

394

395

396

Artist: **PHILIP BLISS**

Art Director: Philip Bliss

Client: American Showcase

Size: 10 x 8

397

Artist: **RON FINGER**

Art Director: Richard Lawrence
Baron

Agency: Quest Business Agency

Medium: Pastel

Size: 23 x 41

398

Artist: **PHIL BOATWRIGHT**

Art Directors: Phil Boatwright
David Spurlock

Client: Society of Illustrators
of Dallas

Medium: Mixed

Size: 12 x 9

399

Artist: **ETIENNE DELESSERT**

Art Director: Etienne Delessert

Client: Musée Des Arts Décoratifs,
Switzerland

Medium: Watercolor

Size: 7 x 5

396

397

398

399

400

Artist: **DAVID BOWERS**

Medium: Oil on gessoed masonite

Size: 14 1/2 x 10 3/4

401

Artist: **KERNE ERICKSON**

Size: 28 x 32

402

Artist: **ALLEN GARNS**

Art Directors: Brad Ghormley
Steve Smit
Art Lofgreen

Client: Messenger Graphics

Medium: Oil

Size: 34 x 26

403

Artist: **W. B. PARK**

Medium: Ink, watercolor

Size: 13 x 10

400

401

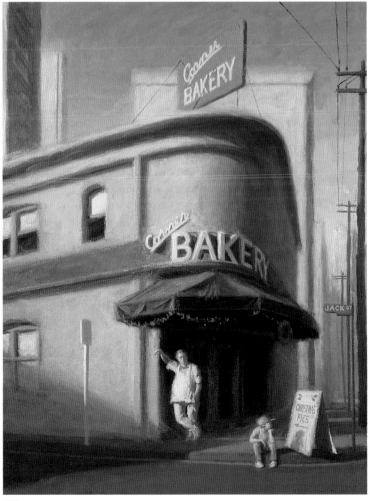

402

403

404

Artist: **DANIEL CRAIG**

Art Director: Dave Peterson

Client: Children's Museum

Medium: Oil

Size: 28 x 23

405

Artist: **ALLEN GARNS**

Art Directors: Brad Ghormley
Steve Smit
Art Lofgreen

Client: Childsplay Theatre

Medium: Oil

Size: 18 x 18

406

Artist: **MARK A.
FREDRICKSON**

Art Director: John Vitro

Agency: Franklin Stoorza

Client: Thermoscan

Medium: Acrylic

Size: 12 x 19

407

Artist: **M. JOHN ENGLISH**

Art Director: Kevin Pistilli

Client: Raphael Hotel Group

Medium: Oil on canvas

Size: 18 x 24

404

405

406

407

408

Artist: **FRED HILLIARD**

Client: Olympus Press

Medium: Pen, ink, gouache

Size: 24 x 18

409

Artist: **JACK UNRUH**

Art Director: Danny Kamerath

Client: Triton Energy Corporation

Size: 13 x 12

410

Artist: **RICHARD WEHRMAN**

Art Director: Jeff Gabel

Agency: Hutchins Y&R

Client: Dresser-Rand

Medium: Acrylic

Size: 11 x 22

411

Artist: **CARLOS TORRES**

Medium: Acrylic, airbrush

Size: 19 x 14

412

Artist: **C. F. PAYNE**

Art Directors: Fred Woodward
              Harold Burch

Agency: Pentagram

Client: Applied Graphic
        Technologies

Medium: Mixed media

Size: 17 1/2 x 13

408

TRITON IS CURRENTLY TESTING A MAJOR OIL DISCOVERY IN the LLANOS BASIN of COLOMBIA. Probably one of the largest finds ever in the WESTERN HEMISPHERE. It's not surprising that TRITON'S a major player there. That's just the kind of company it is. If I had to define TRITON'S year in a phrase it would be...

409

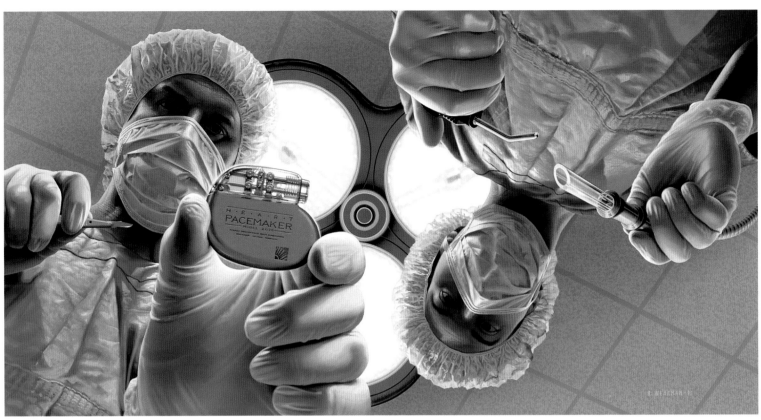

410

411

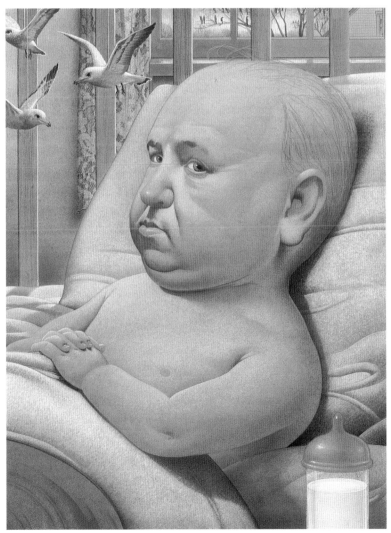

412

413

Artist: **PAUL ROGERS**

Art Director: Brad Stone

Client: Wherehouse Entertainment

Medium: Acrylic

Size: 36 x 22

414

Artist: **WILL WILSON**

Art Director: Sean Delonis

Client: The John Pence Gallery

Medium: Oil

Size: 19 x 14

415

Artist: **EDWARD SOREL**

Art Director: Marcus Ratliff

Client: Susan Conway Galleries

Medium: Pen, watercolor

Size: 13 1/2 x 10

416

Artist: **MARK SUMMERS**

Art Director: Pat Levy

Agency: Hudson Health Care
Communications

Client: Wyeth-Ayerst Laboratories

Medium: Scratchboard, watercolor

Size: 6 1/2 x 8 1/2

414

415

416

417

Artist: **WILL WILLIAMS**

Medium: Oil

Size: 51 x 34

418

Artist: **GREG HARGREAVES**

Client: Hellman Associates

Medium: Acrylic, colored pencil

Size: 16 x 11

419

Artist: **SALLY WERN COMPORT**

Art Director: Tom Nujens

Agency: Robin Shepherd Studio

Client: Blue Cross & Blue Shield of Florida

Medium: Mixed media

Size: 15 x 12

420

Artist: **JOHN H. HOWARD**

Art Director: Bob Dinetz

Client: Metaphor

Medium: Acrylic on canvas

Size: 2' x 6'

417

418

419

420

421

Artist: **SARAH WALDRON**

Size: 10 x 10

422

Artist: **BILL MAYER**

Art Director: D. J. Stout

Client: Texas Monthly

Medium: Airbrush

Size: 15 x 15

423

Artist: **JEFF MEYER**

Art Director: Bill Cook

Agency: William Cook Graphics

Client: Republic Capital Group Inc.

Medium: Pastel, charcoal

Size: 18 1/4 x 11 1/2

424

Artist: **STEVE JOHNSON LOU FANCHER**

Art Director: Karen Geiger

Client: Employee Benefit Plans

Medium: Acrylic on paper

Size: 16 x 13

425

Artist: **RICHARD HARRINGTON**

Art Director: Kathy Cairo

Agency: Buck & Pulleyn

Client: AD Council of Rochester

Size: 13 x 21

421

422

423

424

425

426

Artist: **CHRIS HOPKINS**

Art Director: Chris Hopkins

Client: Fairy Tale Mail

Medium: Oil

Size: 15 1/2 x 11

427

Artist: **MAXINE BOLL**

Art Directors: Maxine Boll
    Melanie Paykos

Client: Los Angeles County
   Museum of Art Council

Size: 21 x 30

428

Artist: **MATT MYERS**

Art Director: Bryan Winke

Client: Florida Winefest

Medium: Oil on board

Size: 36 x 24

429

Artist: **GARY LOCKE**

Art Directors: Matt Key
    Jeff Jansen

Client: Summer Stage

Size: 23 x 14

430

Artist: **BILL MAYER**

Art Director: Steve Russo

Agency: Russo Assoc.

Medium: Airbrush

Size: 8 1/2 x 11 1/2

426

427

428

429

430

431

Artist: **MARK ENGLISH**

Art Director: Bruce Hartmen

Client: Johnson County
Community College

Medium: Oil pastel

Size: 21 x 32

432

Artist: **MARK ENGLISH**

Art Director: Bruce Hartmen

Client: Johnson County
Community College

Medium: Oil pastel

Size: 17 x 23

433

Artist: **MARK A. BENDER**

Art Directors: Vance Wright Adams
Karen Burns

Agency: Vance Wright Adams &
Assoc.

Client: Consolidated Natural
Gas Co.

Medium: Gouache

Size: 31 x 6 1/2

434

Artist: **JOHN F. MARTIN**

Art Director: Les Mintz

Medium: Oil

Size: 17 x 13

435

Artist: **ALAIN MOREAU**

Client: National Park Academy of
the Arts

Medium: Prismacolor

Size: 20 x 15

431

432

433

434

435

436

Artist: **TIM O'BRIEN**

Medium: Oil on gessoed panel

Size: 18 ¹/2 x 17 ¹/2

437

Artist: **LARRY MOORE**

Art Director: Larry Moore

Client: Central Florida Press

Medium: Pastel

Size: 12 x 12

438

Artist: **ALEX MURAWSKI**

Art Director: Akiva Boker

Client: Lasky Printing/Murawski

Medium: Ink, acrylic

Size: 9 x 10 ¹/2

439

Artist: **BILL MAYER**

Art Director: Don Smith

Agency: Adsmith

Medium: Airbrush

Size: 13 ¹/2 x 10 ¹/2

440

Artist: **DAN JONES**

Client: Richard Salzman

Medium: Pencil drawing, airbrush

Size: 15 x 8 ¹/2

436

437

438

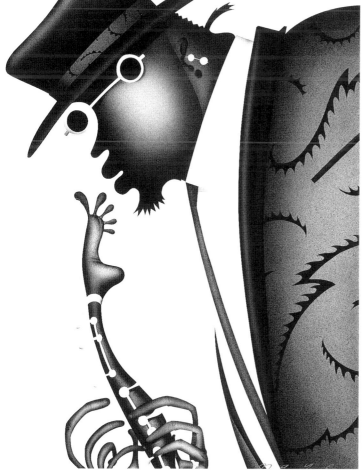

439

440

441

Artist: **JACK UNRUH**

Art Director: Brian Boyd

Size: 17 x 20

442

Artist: **JON ELLIS**

Size: 16 x 19

443

Artist: **RAFAL OLBINSKI**

Art Director: Alane Gehagen

Agency: Ziff Marketing

Client: New York City Opera

Medium: Acrylic on canvas

Size: 32 1/2 x 26

444

Artist: **JOHN P. THOMPSON**

Client: Hellman Associates

Medium: Scratchboard, acrylic

Size: 12 x 9 1/2

445

Artist: **VITO-LEONARDO SCAROLA**

Art Director: Vito-Leonardo Scarola

Client: American Red Cross, Orange County, CA Chapter

Medium: Oil on illustration board

Size: 16 x 23

441

442

443

444

445

446

Artist: **WILSON McLEAN**

Art Director: Roy Comiskey

Client: Security Management

Medium: Oil

Size: 25 x 20

447

Artist: **LELAND KLANDERMAN**

448

Artist: **MARY GRANDPRÉ**

Size: 18 x 10 1/2

449

Artist: **TOM CURRY**

Client: James Conrad

Medium: Acrylic

Size: 14 x 11

450

Artist: **JOHN CRAIG**

Art Director: Dave Willett

Agency: Rhea & Kaiser Advertising, Inc.

Client: Temik

Size: 12 x 9

446

447

448

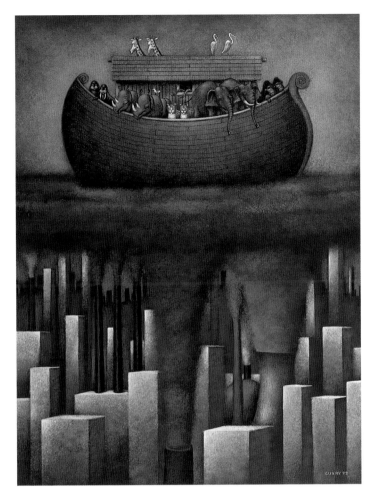

449

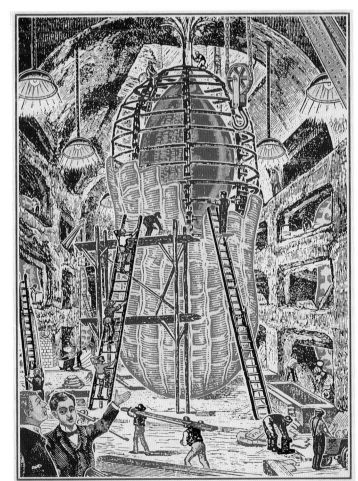

450

451

Artist: **FRANCIS LIVINGSTON**

Client: Open Hand Program

Size: 19 x 24

452

Artist: **PAUL ZWOLAK**

Art Director: Paul Marince

Agency: SlaughterHanson
Advertising

Client: Omni Plan/Sungard

Medium: Oil

Size: 14 x 14

453

Artist: **GARY KELLEY**

Art Director: Pat Levy

Agency: Hudson Health Care
Communications

Client: Wyeth-Ayerst Laboratories

Medium: Pastel

Size: 22 x 28

454

Artist: **CHARLES ROWE**

Medium: Oil, collage

Size: 16 x 12

455

Artist: **FERNANDO RANGEL**

Art Director: Marvin Mattelson

Client: School of Visual Arts

Medium: Oil

Size: 18 x 13

451

452

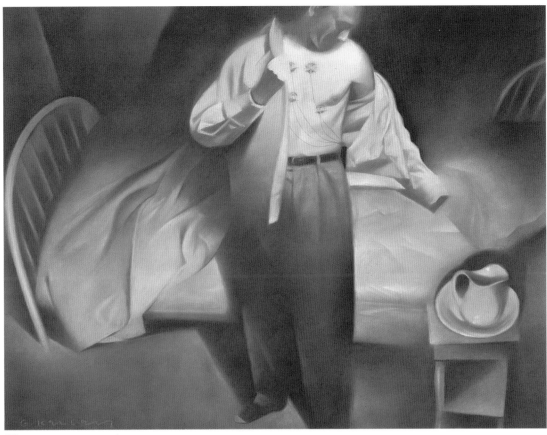

453

454

455

456

Artist: **KAZUHIKO SANO**

Art Director: Kazuhiko Sano

Client: Society of Illustrators
of San Francisco

Medium: Acrylic

Size: 20 x 16

457

Artist: **SUE ROTHER**

Client: Jerry Leff Associates

Size: 15 x 15

458

Artist: **FRANK A. STEINER**

Art Director: Michael Turner

Client: Harleysville Life
Insurance Co.

Size: 19 1/2 x 25 1/2

459

Artist: **DAVID GROFF**

Art Director: Michele Edwards

Client: World Watch Institute

Medium: Mixed media

Size: 15 x 12

460

Artist: **GREG HARGREAVES**

Client: Hellman Associates

Medium: Acrylic, colored pencil

Size: 24 x 20

456

457

458

459

460

461

Artist: **LONNI SUE JOHNSON**

Art Director: Chris Passehl

Client: Wolf Color Print &
Goodspeed Opera House

Medium: Watercolor

Size: 17 x 15

462

Artist: **PAUL ZWOLAK**

Art Director: Paul Marince

Agency: SlaughterHanson
Advertising

Client: Omni Plan/Sungard

Medium: Oil

Size: 13 x 13

463

Artist: **FRANCIS LIVINGSTON**

Art Director: Bill Dunn

Client: Freda Scott

Medium: Oil

Size: 12 x 11

464

Artist: **STEVEN POLSON**

Medium: Oil

Size: 14 x 12

465

Artist: **C. F. PAYNE**

Art Director: Will Hillenbrand

Client: Butler Manufacturing

Medium: Mixed

Size: 11 x 11

461

462

463

464

465

466

Artist: **GREG RUDD**

Art Director: James Helzer

Client: Unicover Corporation

Medium: Oil on gesso and board

Size: 15 x 12

467

Artist: **GREGORY LOUDON**

Medium: Acrylic

Size: 12 ¹/₂ x 18 ¹/₂

468

Artist: **MARK RYDEN**

Art Director: David Bartels

Agency: Bartels Associates

Client: GDS

Medium: Acrylic

Size: 11 x 23

469

Artist: **KEN HAMILTON**

Medium: Watercolor

Size: 9 x 14

470

Artist: **PAUL RATZ DE TAGYOS**

Medium: Oil on masonite

Size: 8 x 12

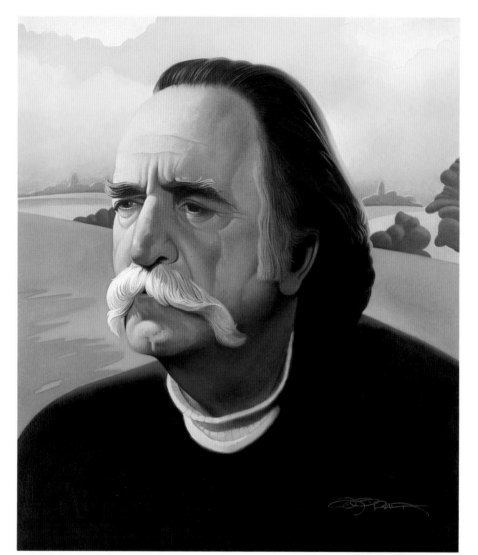

466

467

468

469

470

471

Artist: **BUD KEMPER**

Art Director: Carl Hermann

Client: Maritz, Inc.

Medium: Oil

Size: 24 x 22

472

Artist: **MARK ENGLISH**

Art Director: Bruce Hartmen

Client: Johnson County
    Community College

Medium: Oil, pastel

Size: 20 x 17

473

Artist: **GARY KELLEY**

Art Director: Pat Levy

Agency: Hudson Health Care
    Communications

Client: Wyeth-Ayerst Laboratories

Medium: Pastel

Size: 22 x 28

474

Artist: **JOHN COLLIER**

Art Director: Richard Solomon

Medium: Oil pastel

Size: 36 x 40

475

Artist: **DANIEL SCHWARTZ**

Art Director: Richard Solomon

Medium: Oil

Size: 82 x 64

471

472

473

474

475

476

Artist: **SCOTT HUNT**

Art Director: Ed Giganti

Client: The Catholic Health
Association

Medium: Charcoal

Size: 11 x 13

477

Artist: **PAUL MELIA**

Medium: Ink, gouache, watercolor

Size: 38 x 42

478

Artist: **LARRY WINBORG**

Art Director: Larry Winborg

Client: Sage Publishing

Medium: Oil

Size: 24 x 30

479

Artist: **ROBERT MEGANCK**

Art Director: Robert Meganck

Client: Communication Design,
Inc.

Medium: Scratchboard

Size: 24 x 15 ¹/2

480

Artist: **BUD KEMPER**

Art Director: Carl Hermann

Client: Maritz, Inc.

Medium: Oil

Size: 24 x 22

476

477

478

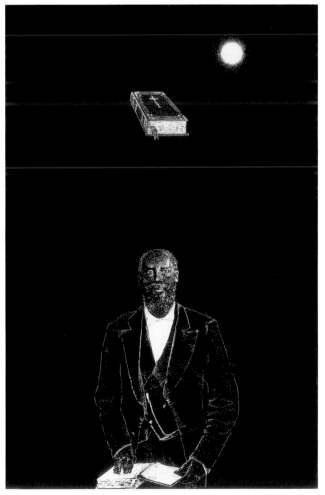

479

480

481

Artist: **DEBORAH L. CHABRIAN**

Art Directors: Lynn Hollyn
Marty Roelandt

Client: Gibson Greetings Inc.

Medium: Watercolor

Size: 11 x 13

482

Artist: **GLENN HARRINGTON**

Art Director: Doug Johnson

Client: Society of Illustrators

Medium: Oil

Size: 22 x 24

483

Artist: **PAUL LACKNER**

Client: Hellman Associates

Medium: Watercolor

Size: 14 x 21

484

Artist: **BRAD HOLLAND**

Art Director: Albert Leutwyler

Client: Joint Ethics Committee

Medium: Acrylic on board

Size: 14 x 11

485

Artist: **RAFAL OLBINSKI**

Client: Andre Zarre Gallery

Size: 31 x 24

481

482

483

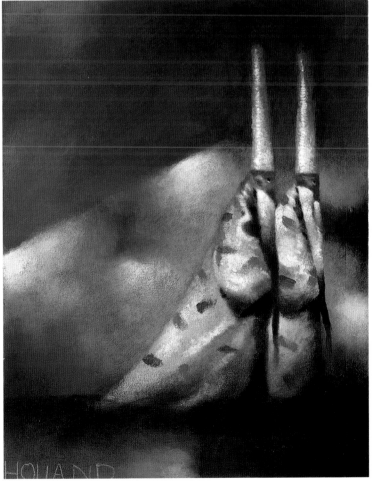

484

485

486

Artist: **DAVID BOWERS**

Medium: Oil on gessoed illustration board

Size: 12 x 10 1/2

487

Artist: **JOHN JINKS**

Art Directors: Elena Foundos
            Robin Presslaff

Client: New York University/SCE

Medium: Acrylic

Size: 19 x 17

488

Artist: **BERNIE FUCHS**

Art Director: Jack Scharr

Client: '92 Olympics

Medium: Oil

Size: 28 x 40

489

Artist: **WILL HILLENBRAND**

Art Director: Bart Crosby

Client: Champion International

Medium: Oil on linen

Size: 20 x 28

486

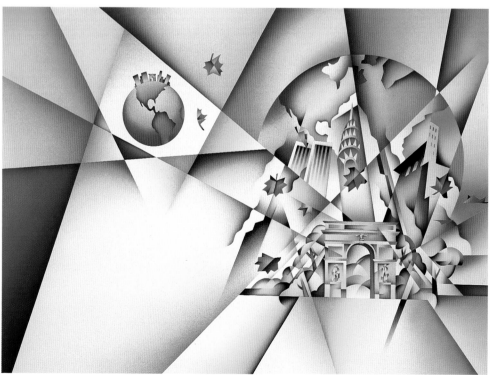

487

488

489

490

Artist: **ROBERT McGINNIS**

Medium: Oil

Size: 11 x 8

491

Artist: **WILSON McLEAN**

Art Director: Bill Shin

Agency: Barton Gillete

Client: University of Michigan
Medical Center

Medium: Oil

Size: 25 1/2 x 18

492

Artist: **ROBERT HUNT**

Client: Barbara Gordon Associates

Size: 31 1/2 x19

493

Artist: **JOEL SPECTOR**

Art Director: Kari Voldeng

Client: St. John's Hospital

Medium: Pastel on canvas

Size: 41 x 72

490

491

492

493

NEW VISIONS

NEW VISIONS

The future of illustration lives in the young artists who test their new-found skills, break away from tradition, and create their own visions. The Society of Illustrators is again pleased to reproduce the catalogue of its Annual Student Scholarship Competition in this year's Annual Book so that you may see illustration from the perspective of these talented young artists.

From the over 5,500 entries received from 100 accredited institutions nationwide, 121 works by young artists were selected by a prestigious jury. Again, Beverly Sacks was instrumental in the crucial fund raising for awards and Alvin Pimsler, Chairman of the Education Committee, guided the jury through the lengthy selection process. The original works were exhibited at the Society of Illustrators Museum of American Illustration.

The technical proficiency and level of problem solving is again exceptional in these young people. It is not difficult to imagine students from across the country entering the marketplace with the tools necessary to achieve success.

We hope you will enjoy the promise of the future in New Visions.

Congratulations to all those involved in the 1993 Student Scholarship Competition.

Those students whose work has been accepted into this exhibition can be *very* proud of their great accomplishments, and those who are award winners can be doubly proud. It's an exceptional achievement. A special commendation to the families of these students for their unequaled and invaluable support. This is a great tribute to you as well.

Congratulations also go to the colleges who continue to uphold their highest standards and to their instructors who inspire, encourage, guide and share their professional expertise with the students through their formative years.

Special thanks go the Hallmark Corporate Foundation for its truly generous funding over the years and to those sponsors who continue to encourage students with their invaluable support, including The Starr Foundation, The Reader's Digest Association, Jellybean Photographics, The Franklin Mint Foundation for the Arts, Dick Blick Art Materials and Hachette Magazines; and plaudits to Alvin Pimsler, Chairman of our Education Committee for his superb work on behalf of the students, the 16 judges who also devoted so much of their valuable time and efforts in this undertaking; and to Beverly Sacks, Chairperson of our Annual Christmas Auction, which brings in major funding for our scholarship programs each year.

Supporting our future generation is one of the most rewarding and gratifying efforts one can possibly make and so our gratitude goes out to all involved in this endeavor.

And finally, there's a long, hard road ahead of you, students, but the rewards are great and the profession is one of the finest and most satisfying in the world.

Continued success and prosperity to you all.

Eileen Hedy Schultz
President

Each year the scholarship exhibition, sponsored by the Society of Illustrators, continues to provide fresh, new talent for the professional field of illustration. This year is no exception. The work on display in the exhibition gallery at the Society, and in this catalogue, is as usual at the highest standard.

The students who came through the trial of submitting, selection and the awards, should be justifiably proud; as should their parents and teachers who gave them sincere and solid support. The Society of Illustrators is pleased to be the conduit presenting the marketplace the opportunity to view the new and promising work offered by these young people.

Congratulations to these future professionals and their parents and teachers. The Society's special thanks to the jurors, who worked so hard and fairly, and gave so freely of their time.

Alvin J. Pimsler
Chairman, Education Committee

▶
Sean Beavers
Marvin Mattelson, Instructor
School of Visual Arts
$2,000 Robert H. Blattner Award

Tonya Fisher
Susanne Spann, Instructor
Ringling School of Art and Design
$1,500 Dick Blick Art Materials Award

Ian Graham
Joel Nakamura, Instructor
Art Center College of Design
$1,500
The Reader's Digest Association Award

Michael Fadollone
David Mocarski, Instructor
Art Center College of Design
$1,500
The Reader's Digest Association Award

▶
Dean Kube
Mark Langeneckert, Instructor
Kansas City Art Institute
$1,500 The Starr Foundation Award

▼
Steven Knotts
David Mocarski, Instructor
Art Center College of Design
$1,500 Jellybean Photographics Award

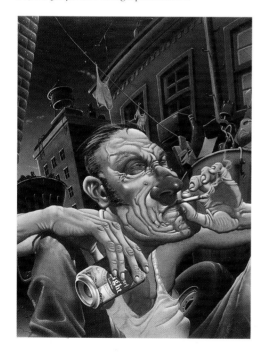

▲
Nicole Tortoriello
Phyllis Purves-Smith, Instructor
University of the Arts
$1,500
The Franklin Mint Foundation
for the Arts Award

◄
Kosal Kong
Paul Kratter, Instructor
Academy of Art College
$1,500 The Starr Foundation Award

►
Krista Wallhagen
Jack de Graffenried, Instructor
Sacred Heart University
$1,500 Jellybean Photographics Award

▼
Joan Costello
Peter Caras, Instructor
duCret School of the Arts
$1,000
Norma and Alvin Pimsler Award

▲
Maria Somma
Rosemary Torre, Instructor
Fashion Institute of Technology
$1,000 The Starr Foundation Award

▶

Kimberlee Lynch
Jon McDonald, Instructor
Kendall College of Art & Design
$1,000 The Starr Foundation Award

▼

Victor Zavala
Larry Johnson, Instructor
California State University
at Fullerton
$1,000
The Reader's Digest Association Award

▼

Daisuke Takeya
Frances Jetter/Linda Benson,
Instructors
School of Visual Arts
$1,000 Hachette Filipacchi
Magazines, Inc. Award

◀
David Dedman
John Falato, Instructor
Paier College of Art
$750
The Reader's Digest Association Awa

▶
Paul Lachapelle
Benton Mahan, Instructor
Columbus College of Art & Design
$750 Phillips/Rodewig Award

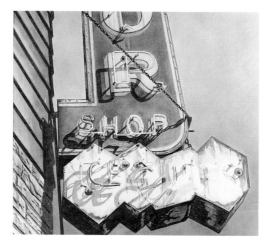

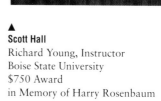

▲
Scott Hall
Richard Young, Instructor
Boise State University
$750 Award
in Memory of Harry Rosenbaum

▲
Wendy Mersman
Jon McDonald, Instructor
Kendall College of Art & Design
$750 Award
in Memory of Robert Anthony

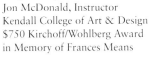

Craig Pennington
Jon McDonald, Instructor
Kendall College of Art & Design
$750 Kirchoff/Wohlberg Award
in Memory of Frances Means

▼
Christopher Petrocchi
Courtney Granner, Instructor
San Jose State University
$750 Award
in Memory of Meg Wohlberg

▲
Charles Wren
Peter Caras, Instructor
duCret School of the Arts
$750 Award
in Memory of D.L. Cramer

▲
Mari Lou Smith
Barbara Pearlman, Instructor
Fashion Institute of Technology
$750 Award
in Memory of Jim Dickerson

▲
J. Chadwick Cameron
Durwood Dommisse, Instructor
Virginia Commonwealth University
$500 Award

▲
Michael Petit
Charles Rowe, Instructor
Univeristy of Delaware
$500 Award

▲
Nanci Geideman
Roy Waits, Instructor
ACA College of Design
$500 Award

▼
Robert Sullivan
Marvin Mattelson, Instructor
School of Visual Arts
$500 Award

▲
Matt Manley
Jon McDonald, Instructor
Kendall College of Art & Design
$500 Award

▼
Gwenda Kaczor
Chris Polentz, Instructor
Art Center College of Design
$500 Award

▲
Cyndi Grill
Jon McDonald, Instructor
Kendall College of Art & Design
$500 Award

▼
David Gianfredi
Jon McDonald, Instructor
Kendall College of Art & Design
$250 Award

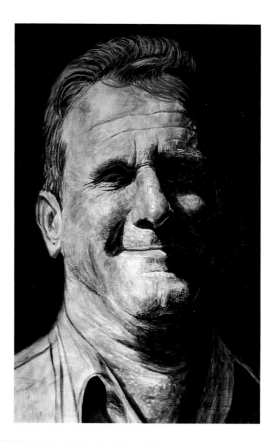

▶
Tony Terrell
George Fernandez, Instructor
Long Island University at C.W. Post
$250 Award

▲
Robert Moody
Thomas Sgouros, Instructor
Rhode Island School of Design
$250 Award

▶
Joel Parod
Eve Page, Instructor
San Jose State University
$250 Award

▼
Brian Blood
Craig Nelson, Instructor
Academy of Art College
$100 Award

▲
Laura Cronin
Jack Endewelt, Instructor
School of Visual Arts
$100 Award

◄
Julia Lundman
Rich Kryczka, Instructor
American Academy of Art
$100 Award

◄
Randsom Owens
Glen Edwards, Instructor
Utah State University
$100 Award

▲
Eric Nava
Craig Nelson, Instructor
Academy of Art College
$100 Award

3

5

1

2

4

9

10

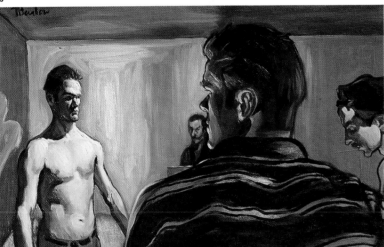

6

8

7

THE EXHIBIT

11

Addiction

12

20

15

17

16

18

14

19

13

21

24

22

25

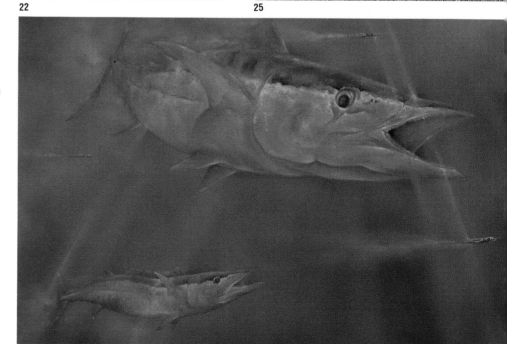

23

26

29

30

27

28

31

33

38

40

34

35

39

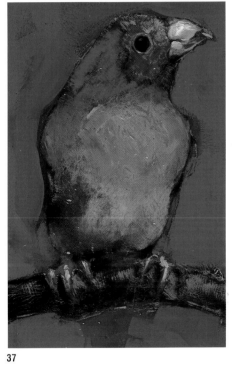

37

32

36

41

42

49

45

47

51

50

43

48

46

44

56

53

62

54

57

58

59

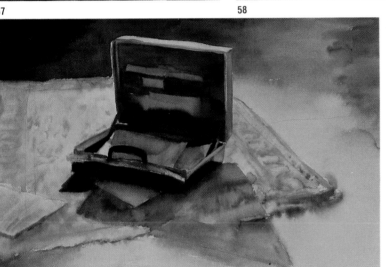

52

60

61

55

65

71

63

68

70

66

64

69

72

67

73

77

76

75

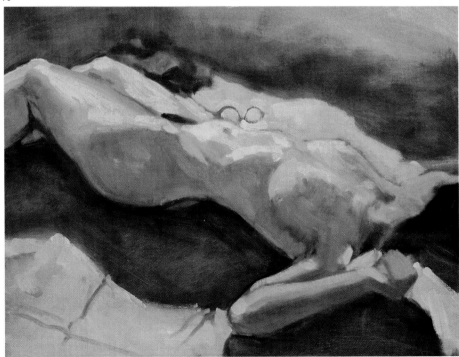

74

78

82

81

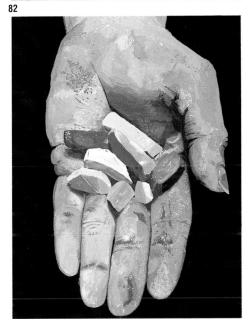

79

83

80

ARTIST INDEX

Filip, Traian Alexandru, 388
111 Aquetong Rd.
New Hope, PA 18938
(215) 862-0320

Finger, Ron, 353, 356, 372, 397
7798 Platt Ave. NW
South Haven, MN 55382
(612) 236-7600

Fiore, Peter, 54
PO Box 279
Matamoras, PA 18336
(717) 491-5002

Flesher, Vivienne, 320, 382
c/o Vicki Morgan
194 3rd Ave.
New York, NY 10003
(212) 475-0440

Forbes, Bart, 275, 305
5323 Montrose Dr.
Dallas, TX 75209
(214) 357-8077

Frazier, Craig, 262
600 Townsend St. #412W
San Francisco, CA 94103
(415) 863-9613

Fredrickson, Mark A., 311, 406
853 S. Pantano Pky.
Tucson, AZ 85710
(602) 722-5777

Fuchs, Bernie, 263, 277, 314, 488
3 Tanglewood Lane
Westport, CT 06880
(203) 227-4644

Gallagher, Saelig, 120
3624 Amaryllis Dr.
San Diego, CA 92106
(619) 224-6313

Garcia, Manuel, 167
716 Sanchez St.
San Francisco, CA 94114
(415) 285-8267

Garland, Michael, 375
19 Manor Rd., RR#2
Patterson, NY 12563
(914) 878-4347

Garns, Allen, 402, 405
209 W. First Ave.
Mesa, AZ 85210
(602) 835-5769

Gauthier, Corbert, 332
4073 Utica Ave. South
St. Louis Park, MN 55416
(612) 926-1096

Gersten, Gerry, 336
177 Newtown Tpke.
Weston, CT 06883
(203) 222-1608

Giusti, Robert, 16, 379
340 Long Mountain Rd.
New Milford, CT 06776
(203) 354-6539

Gosfield, Josh, 371
682 Broadway #105
New York, NY 10012
(212) 254-2582

Grandpré, Mary, 257, 448
475 Cleveland Ave. N.
St. Paul, MN 55104
(612) 645-3463

Graves, Keith, 8
905 W. 29
Austin, TX 78705
(512) 478-3338

Griesbach/Martucci, 294
41 Lighthouse Rd.
Highlands, NJ 07732
(908) 291-5945

Groff, David, 459
420 N. Liberty St.
Delaware, OH 43015
(614) 363-2131

Hagio, Kunio, 41
125 Table Top Rd.
Sedona, AZ 86336
(602) 282-3574

Hamilton, Ken, 469
16 Helen Ave.
W. Orange, NJ 07052
(201) 736-6532

Hargreaves, Greg, 418, 460
414 Cornwall Ave.
Waterloo, IA 50702
(319) 233-7573

Harrington, Glenn, 14, 347, 482
329 Twin Lear Rd.
Pipersville, PA 18947
(215) 294-8109

Harrington, Richard, 425
87 N. Clinton, #417
Rochester, NY 14604
(716) 262-4571

Hawkes, Kevin, 204
30 Central Ave.
Peaks Island, ME 04108
(207) 766-5153

Haymans, Traci, 239
88 Broad Reach Ct.
Savannah, GA 31410
(912) 897-0902

Head, Gary, 188
6023 Wyandotte
Kansas City, MO 64113
(816) 363-3119

Henderson, Garnet, 110, 126
820 Hudson
Hoboken, NJ 07030
(201) 653-3948

Hillenbrand, Will, 489
808 Lexington Ave.
Terrace Park, OH 45174
(513) 831-5830

Hilliard, Fred, 312, 408
5425 Crystal Springs
Bainbridge Island, WA 98110
(206) 842-6003

Holland, Brad, 17, 69, 107, 484
96 Greene St.
New York, NY 10012
(212) 226-3675

Hooks, Mitchell, 176
321 E. 83rd St.
New York, NY 10028
(212) 737-1853

Hopkins, Chris, 253, 426
5018 Sound Ave.
Everett, WA 98203
(206) 347-5613

Howard, John H., 211, 420
336 E. 54th St.
New York, NY 10020
(212) 832-7980

Huerta, Catherine, 198
337 W. 20th St., #4M
New York, NY 10011

Hunt, Robert, 218, 251, 301, 492
107 Crescent Rd.
San Anselmo, CA 94960
(415) 459-6882

Hunt, Scott, 476
6 Charles St.
New York, NY 10014
(212) 924-1105

Hynes, Robert, 175, 186
512 Muncaster Mill Rd.
Rockville, MD 20855
(301) 926-7813

James, Derek, 205
262 Fording Place Rd.
Lake Katrine, NY 12449
(914) 336-2629

Jensen, Bruce, 228
41-61 53rd St.
Woodside, NY 11377
(718) 898-1887

Jessell, Tim, 298
1906 Wedgewood Ct.
Stillwater, OK 74075
(405) 377-3619

Jetter, Frances, 259
390 West End Ave.
New York, NY 10024
(212) 580-3720

Jinks, John, 487
27 W. 20th St., #1106
New York, NY 10011
(212) 675-2961

Johnson, David, 28, 58, 173
299 South Ave.
New Canaan, CT 06840
(203) 966-3269

Johnson, Joel Peter, 52, 170, 264
PO Box 803, Ellicott Station
Buffalo, NY 14205
(716) 881-1757

Johnson, Lonni Sue, 461
310 W. 72nd St., PH #3
New York, NY 10023
(212) 873-7749

Johnson, Stephen T., 189, 225
81 Remsen St. #1
Brooklyn, NY 11201
(718) 237-2352

Johnson, Steve, 115, 424
440 Sheridan Ave. So.
Minneapolis, MN 55405
(612) 377-8728

Jones, Dan, 440
3629 Georgia St.
San Diego, CA 92103
(619) 294-9255

Joyce, William, 226
3302 Centenary Blvd.
Shreveport, LA 71104

Kabrin, Carole, 90
1300 Porter, Apt. 50
Dearborn, MI 48124
(313) 561-7291

Kawakami, Natsumi, 292
1041-11 Tamado
Shimodate City, Ibaraki-Pref., 308
Japan
(011) 81-296-28-2920

Kecman, Milan, 286
4736 S. Hills Dr., S.W.
Cleveland, OH 44109
(216) 741-8755

Kelley, Gary, 78, 118, 133,
    453, 473
301 1/2 Main St.
Cedar Falls, IA 50613
(319) 277-2330

Kemper, Bud, 471, 480
52 High Trail
Eureka, MO 63025
(314) 938-4122

Klanderman, Leland, 370, 447
Oasis Art Co.
118 E. 26th St.
Minneapols, MN 55405
(612) 871-4539

Klauba, Douglas C., 89
233 E. Ontario, Suite 901
Chicago, IL 60611
(312) 943-4676

Klein, Christopher A., 70
c/o National Geographic
1145 17th St. NW
Washington, DC 20036

Laager, Ken, 192, 209, 212
304 North Elm St.
Lititz, PA 17543
(717) 627-2085

Labbé, John, 21, 97
97 Third Ave.
New York, NY 10003
(212) 529-2831

Lackner, Paul, 483
422 2nd St. S.E.
Waverly, IA 50677
(319) 352-5689

Landikusic, Katherine, 49, 258
4649 Stateline Rd.
Kansas City, MO 64112
(816) 753-2247

Larkin, Bob, 169
10 Bluebell Lane
Northport, NY 11768
(516) 261-4495

Lee, Victor, 345
1633 California St. #114
San Francisco, CA 94109
(415) 775-3613

Leister, Bryan, 116, 157
202 E. Raymond Ave.
Alexandria, VA 22301
(703) 683-1544

Lesh, David, 350
5693 N. Meridian St.
Indianapolis, IN 46208
(317) 253-3141

Lewis, H. B., 22
119 Benefit St. #5
Providence, RI 02903
(401) 272-6922

Lewis, Maurice, 360
3704 Harper St.
Houston, TX 77005
(713) 664-1807

Lewis, Tim, 276
184 St. Johns Place
Brooklyn, NY 11217-3402

Liepke, Skip, 2, 40, 102, 103, 322
30 W. 72nd St. #2B
New York, NY 10023
(212) 724-5593

Lindlof, Ed, 241
603 Carolyn Ave.
Austin, TX 78705
(512) 472-0195

Linn, Warren, 281
4915 Broadway, #2A
New York, NY 10034
(212) 942-6383

Livingston, Francis, 269, 363,
    451, 463
19 Brookmont Cir.
San Anselmo, CA 94960
(415) 456-7103

ART DIRECTORS, CLIENTS, AGENCIES

PROFESSIONAL STATEMENTS

GERALD & CULLEN RAPP

Illustration

RAY AMEIJIDE	LASZLO KUBINYI
EMMANUEL AMIT	SHARMEN LIAO
GARY BASEMAN	LEE LORENZ
LOU BORY ASSOCIATES	BERNARD MAISNER
MICHAEL DAVID BROWN	ALLAN MARDON
LON BUSCH	HAL MAYFORTH
JOSE CRUZ	BRUCE MORSER
JACK DAVIS	ALEX MURAWSKI
BOB DESCHAMPS	MARLIES NAJAKA
BILL DEVLIN	BOB PETERS
LEE DUGGAN	SIGMUND PIFKO
THE DYNAMIC DUO	JERRY PINKNEY
JACKI GELB	CAMILLE PRZEWODEK
RANDY GLASS	MARC ROSENTHAL
THOMAS HART	DREW STRUZAN
CELIA JOHNSON	MICHAEL WITTE
LIONEL KALISH	CRAIG ZUCKERMAN
ROMEO EMPIRE DESIGN	

108 EAST 35 STREET (#7) NEW YORK, NY 10016
PHONE (212)889-3337 FAX (212)889-3341

Limax maximus

GREAT SLUG

DUGALD STERMER

Represented by Jim Lilie 415-441-4384

Edward Koren
Cartoonist and Illustrator
Pratt '64

Pratt distinguishes you.

©1992 Art work courtesy of Edward Koren.

For over a century, Pratt Institute has helped people distinguish themselves in virtually every creative field. From fine arts to architecture, from photography to computer graphics, Pratt nurtures and motivates students to take their talents as far as they will go.
That's why Pratt students don't just draw it or build it. They also make it.

Pratt
Draw it. Build it. Make it.

PRATT INSTITUTE • 200 Willoughby Ave., Brooklyn, NY 11205 • (718) 636-3669, ext 838 or 1-800-331-0834, ext. 838
PRATT MANHATTAN • 295 Lafayette St., New York, NY 10012 • (212) 925-8481, ext 838
Undergraduate and Graduate Degree Programs • 2-Year Associate Degree Programs • Professional Studies/Continuing Education

Tim O'Brien

LOTT REPRESENTATIVES
212·953·7088

Illustrators

NAME	COLLEGE	NAME	COLLEGE	NAME	COLLEGE
Kelly Alder	School of Visual Arts	John Genzo	School of Visual Arts	Gary Paolillo	School of Visual Arts
Kelynn Alder	School of Visual Arts	Roy Germon	School of Visual Arts	Michael Paraskevas	School of Visual Arts
Dale Allen	School of Visual Arts	Bill Gibbons	School of Visual Arts	Lisa Peet	School of Visual Arts
Ray Alma	School of Visual Arts	Roby Gilbert	School of Visual Arts	Francesca Pelaggi	School of Visual Arts
Matthew Archambault	School of Visual Arts	Lucy Gould-Reitzfeld	School of Visual Arts	Donna Perrone	School of Visual Arts
Gil Ashby	School of Visual Arts	Alexa Grace	School of Visual Arts	Patrick Pigott	School of Visual Arts
Beth Bartholomew	School of Visual Arts	Julie Granahan	School of Visual Arts	Brian Pinkney	School of Visual Arts
Jill Batelman	School of Visual Arts	Cheryl Griesbach	School of Visual Arts	Leticia Plate	School of Visual Arts
James Bennett	School of Visual Arts	Bob Guglielmo	School of Visual Arts	Joel Popadics	School of Visual Arts
Winston Berkel Jr.	School of Visual Arts	Russell Gundlach	School of Visual Arts	Katherine Potter	School of Visual Arts
Rose Mary Berlin	School of Visual Arts	Joseph Gyurcsak	School of Visual Arts	Joe Quesada	School of Visual Arts
Drew Bishop	School of Visual Arts	Kenneth Harrison	School of Visual Arts	Joyce Raimondo	School of Visual Arts
John Boppert	School of Visual Arts	Edward Heck	School of Visual Arts	Chris Reed	School of Visual Arts
Joseph Borzotta	School of Visual Arts	Garnet Henderson	School of Visual Arts	Richard Rehbein	School of Visual Arts
Robert Brennan II	School of Visual Arts	Kingman Huie	School of Visual Arts	Missy Rehfuss	School of Visual Arts
James Cardillo	School of Visual Arts	Richard Hunt	School of Visual Arts	Denise Rettmer	School of Visual Arts
Roger Caruana	School of Visual Arts	Clifford Jackson	School of Visual Arts	Kurt Ritta	School of Visual Arts
Robert Casilla	School of Visual Arts	Donald Jones	School of Visual Arts	Sandro Rodorigo	School of Visual Arts
Andrew Castrucci	School of Visual Arts	Rodney Jung	School of Visual Arts	Barbara Roman	School of Visual Arts
Joseph Cipri	School of Visual Arts	Holly Kaufman-Spruch	School of Visual Arts	Pres Romanillos	School of Visual Arts
Howard Coale	School of Visual Arts	Thomas Kerr	School of Visual Arts	Joseph Rutt	School of Visual Arts
Alan E. Cober	School of Visual Arts	David Klehm	School of Visual Arts	Amantha Samatis	School of Visual Arts
Paul Cozzolino	School of Visual Arts	Norman Kraig	School of Visual Arts	Melinda Saminski	School of Visual Arts
Janelle Cromwell	School of Visual Arts	Mark Lang	School of Visual Arts	Barbara Samuels	School of Visual Arts
Peter Cunis	School of Visual Arts	Russell Lehman	School of Visual Arts	Peter Savigny	School of Visual Arts
Dave Cutler	School of Visual Arts	Marie Lessard	School of Visual Arts	Thomas Sciacca	School of Visual Arts
Joseph Danisi	School of Visual Arts	David Levinson	School of Visual Arts	Mary Servillo	School of Visual Arts
Paul Davis	School of Visual Arts	Mirriam Lippman	School of Visual Arts	Maurice Sherman	School of Visual Arts
William Denoyelles	School of Visual Arts	Missy Longo-Lewis	School of Visual Arts	Susan Sherman-Jackson	School of Visual Arts
Lisa DePolo-Passen	School of Visual Arts	Janie Lowe	School of Visual Arts	Phillip Singer	School of Visual Arts
Diana Deutermann-McKee	School of Visual Arts	Joanne Maffia-Pampinella	School of Visual Arts	Brigitte Sleiertin	School of Visual Arts
Grace DeVito	School of Visual Arts	Kam Mak	School of Visual Arts	Jeffrey Smith	School of Visual Arts
Linda DeVito Soltis	School of Visual Arts	John Mandato	School of Visual Arts	Mark Sparacio	School of Visual Arts
Susan Diehl-Marx	School of Visual Arts	Richard Martin	School of Visual Arts	Dalia Spina	School of Visual Arts
Steve Dininno	School of Visual Arts	Emily Martindale	School of Visual Arts	John Stadler	School of Visual Arts
Eric Dinyer	School of Visual Arts	Sam Martine	School of Visual Arts	Steven Stankiewicz	School of Visual Arts
Maria Dominguez	School of Visual Arts	Stanley Martucci	School of Visual Arts	Deborah Steins	School of Visual Arts
Deborah Dorton	School of Visual Arts	Deborah Max	School of Visual Arts	Dan Stern	School of Visual Arts
Erin Dwyer	School of Visual Arts	Kevin McCloskey	School of Visual Arts	Bruce Strachan	School of Visual Arts
Masako Ebata	School of Visual Arts	Patrick McDonnell	School of Visual Arts	John Stundis	School of Visual Arts
Timothy Ebneth	School of Visual Arts	Lisa McLeod	School of Visual Arts	James Sullivan	School of Visual Arts
Tristan Elwell	School of Visual Arts	Diane Merkel-Shanian	School of Visual Arts	Thomas Thorspecken	School of Visual Arts
Jack Endewelt	School of Visual Arts	Randi Meyerson-Adler	School of Visual Arts	Jeffrey Tomaka	School of Visual Arts
Joanne Farkas	School of Visual Arts	Frances Middendorf	School of Visual Arts	Dorian Vallejo	School of Visual Arts
Teresa Fasolino	School of Visual Arts	Arthur Miller	School of Visual Arts	Eric Velasquez	School of Visual Arts
George Fernandez	School of Visual Arts	Elizabeth Montalvo-Meletiche	School of Visual Arts	Damon Von Eiff	School of Visual Arts
James Forman	School of Visual Arts	Alison Moritsugu	School of Visual Arts	John Ward	School of Visual Arts
Lynne Foster	School of Visual Arts	David Moyers	School of Visual Arts	Lisa Weinblatt	School of Visual Arts
Christine Francis	School of Visual Arts	Joel Naprstek	School of Visual Arts	Joanna Whitney	School of Visual Arts
Douglas Fraser	School of Visual Arts	Emilya Naymark	School of Visual Arts	Mick Wieland	School of Visual Arts
Drew Friedman	School of Visual Arts	Jose Ortega	School of Visual Arts	Joe Wilkonski	School of Visual Arts
Frank Frisari	School of Visual Arts	Felix Padron	School of Visual Arts	Marc Yankus	School of Visual Arts
Patricia Garafano	School of Visual Arts	Richard Pagano	School of Visual Arts	Jonathan Zack	School of Visual Arts
Cynthia Garrett-Maurice	School of Visual Arts	Donna Pallotta	School of Visual Arts	Lynn Zollin	School of Visual Arts
Lee Gaskins III	School of Visual Arts			Darryl Zudeck	School of Visual Arts

Illustration Alumni

School of Visual Arts

①②③ A COLLEGE OF THE ARTS • 209 EAST 23RD STREET • NEW YORK, NEW YORK 10010-3994 • (212) 679-7350 • FAX (212) 725-3587

San Francisco Ballet/Nutcracker

Work in Progress

Minolta/Maybe the Best Way to Handle Risk is to Avoid it Altogether

GTE North Classic/Giants of Golf - Ray Floyd

JERRY LOFARO

57 Laight St. 4th Flr. N.Y., N.Y 10013   (212) 941-7936   Represented By American Artists: (212) 682-2462

For Additional Work, Please See American Showcase 14-17, Society of Illustrators 29, 32- 35 and Communication Arts Annual 34.

These images were photographed using the patented lighting system of Gamma One Conversions Inc. which insures full tonal response at the same contrast as the art. Textural details and brush stroke information are recorded with unprecedented accuracy. Jerry LoFaro uses Gamma One Conversions exclusively for reproduction. Gamma One Conversions Inc. We Make Photographing Art an Art. Contact Maia Nero/212 925-5778

ROSEKRANS HOFFMAN

TOM LEONARD

COLIN BOOTMAN

Kirchoff/Wohlberg, Inc. • 897 Boston Post Road • Madison, CT 06443 • (203) 245-7308

TROY VISS

DANIEL MORETON

KIRCHOFF
WOHLBERG

Artists Representatives

866 United Nations Plaza
New York, NY 10017
(212) 644-2020

THIS IS YOUR WAKE-UP CALL!

The award-winning faculty of The Savannah College of Art and Design illustration department bring extensive professional experience to the classroom. With emphasis on career preparation, the faculty teach and direct students through realistic classroom assignments, new and traditional techniques, and conceptual thinking. If you are ready to rise and shine in the field, check us out.

Earning a degree in Illustration from The Savannah College of Art and Design is something to crow about.

Top to bottom: Dennis Vernon, Ralph Sanders, Traci Haymans, Don Rogers, Julie Mueller-Brown. Center: Dick Krepel

Bachelor of Fine Arts • Master of Fine Arts

Savannah College of Art and Design

Post Office Box 3146 • Savannah, Georgia 31402-3146 • Telephone (912) 238-2483 • Fax (912) 238-2456

Les Paul & Mary Ford in home Studio
Circa 1954

JOE CIARDIELLO   **(718) 727 - 4757**

Right after you get it, it starts to turn yellow.

No wonder. Every art director in the business looks for artists in the same place. They turn to the yellowed pages of Showcase Illustration.

A M E R I C A N   S H O W C A S E

DAVID BOWERS

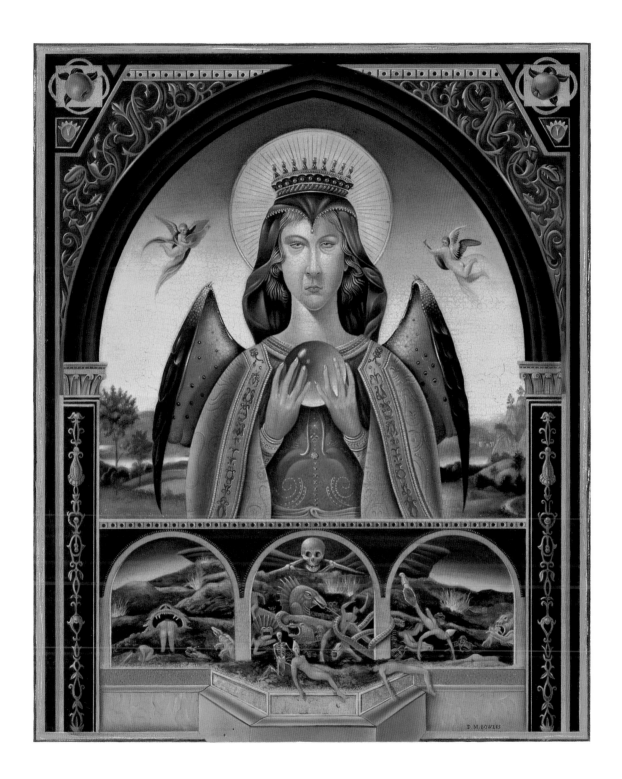

CLIFF‣KNECHT
ARTIST REPRESENTATIVE

309 WALNUT ROAD PITTSBURGH, PA 15202   PHONE 412 • 761 • 5666 FAX 412 • 261 • 3712

We are proud to introduce a very simple way to look at a few of our award-winning illustrators from around the planet. Since words alone can't describe their stellar work, we had to go about showing it in our own colorful way. One that you'll appreciate the first time you open our new 1994 annual. When you do, you'll be at a loss for words, too. Call us at 212-682-1490.

Bernstein & Andriulli.
International Illustration.

MARK FREDRICKSON

6 0 2 • 7 2 2 • 5 7 7 7

Kazuhiko Sano
Studio (415) 381-6377   Fax (415) 381-3847

New York:

Renard Represents Inc.
(212) 490-2450
Fax (212) 697-6828

The Best of Illustration

East 800-322-3470   Midwest 800-752-0285   South 800-346-5266   West 800-547-2688

Tom Nachreiner

illustration

Represented in the Midwest by Art Factory
call Tom Stocki – Telephone 414 785-1940

The House of Portfolios Co. Inc.

Manufacturer & Sales of Fine Hand Made Portfolios

CUSTOM MADE FOR UNIQUE INDIVIDUALS   HAND CRAFTED TO PERFECTION   FOR UNSURPASSED QUALITY

The House of Portfolios Co., Inc.   **Tel. (212) 206-7323   FAX (212) 633-2247**   52 West 21st Street New York, NY 100

GRAPHIC ARTISTS GUILD'S

DIRECTORY OF ILLUSTRATION

More than 21,000 creatives will be using the Directory of Illustration #11 to hire in 1994. The Directory of Illustration delivers results and value for our advertiser.

Pages cost as little as $2050 and include up to 5 color images. Call us today to find out how you can make the Directory of Illustration work for you!

"My association with the Directory goes back several years. Previous to that, my business was mostly word of mouth. I managed to survive, but after advertising in the Directory, my business took a major leap upward. I realized this was the only way to go. It exposed me to more markets than I could have approached on my own."
Michael McGurl

"It's been a pleasure to work with Mike McGurl from "Day One." He has a style that truly stands out on the printed page and has a wonderful feel for color. He's met all our deadlines with room to spare and couldn't be more accommodating. We're working with him on a campaign based on three illustrations, and can't wait until we can enter them into the award shows. Best of all, the first ad has hit the magazines and our client is getting rave reviews from everyone who sees it!"
Sincerely,
Chez Pari, Art Director/SSD&W

ARTIST: Michael McGurl
CLIENT: Besselaar
ART DIRECTOR: Chez Pari
A.D. COMPANY: SSD&W
MEDIUM: Airbrush and Acrylic
SIZE: 14"x15"

EARLY RESERVATION:	MARCH 18, 1994
REGULAR RESERVATION:	APRIL 22, 1994
ARTWORK DUE:	MAY 23, 1994
PUBLICATION DATE:	NOVEMBER 1994

PUBLISHED BY

SERBIN COMMUNICATIONS

511 OLIVE STREET, SANTA BARBARA, CA 93101   805 963-0439   FAX 805 965-0496

New Artists

TRACY SABIN

PAUL COZZOLINO

MARC MONGEAU

WALDEMAR SWIERZY

MARLENA TORZECKA • 211 EAST 89 STREET • SUITE A-1 • NEW YORK • NEW YORK 10128 • TELEPHONE 212 • 289 • 5514

So the world isn't beating a path to your door

just because you have tha

wonder okay, how do I get from here to actually

Cindy Sandro| *illustrator*

being

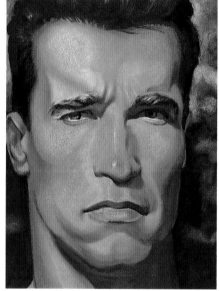

That's where we come in.

some of

the brightest young art directors

Sarah Kennedy| *illustrator*

the country. It's real world experience, taught by

Ruth Mitchell| *illustrator*

program designed to help you create a seasoned,

professiona

Barb Hogan| *illustrator*

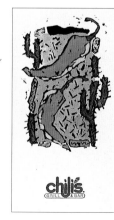

Margaret DeNeergaard| *illustrator*

chili's
GRILL & BAR

hard-earned BFA. And you're  starting to

 illustrator instead of someone who can draw.

Jack Meacham| *illustrator*

Robin Sawyer| *illustrator*

Sheryl Southern| *illustrator*

At Portfolio Center we'll put you to  work with

graphic designers,  photo-  graphers and writers in

Jack Meacham| *illustrator*

Barbara Hogan|*illustrator*

nationally-known, working professionals. A two year

Cindy Sandro| *illustrator*

 portfolio. To make you an illustrator.

David Kacmarynski|*illustrator*

PORTFOLIO
CENTER

125 Bennett Street
Atlanta, Georgia 30309

CALL 1-800-255-3169 FOR OUR FREE CATALOG

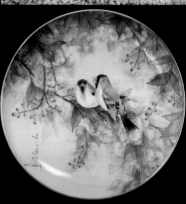

Jim Spanfeller

(914) 232-3546

60 Mustato Road, Katonah, NY 10536

"Best of Saki"
H.H. Munro
Franklin Library
A.D. Michael Mendelsohn

Linotype Machine Promotion Art for The Spanfeller Press
Brewster, New York *A.D. Robert I. York*

"**An American Original** . . .
You can tell a Spanfeller from across the
room. I think it is hard not to be alter-
nately charmed and dazzled by the
work of this gifted artist. The quality is
there, the originality, the impact.
He is distinctive."
Peter Dzwonkoski. Head, Department
of Rare Books and Special Collections,
University of Rochester Library.

Self Portrait

Impossible Vacation, by Spalding Gray • Playboy Magazine • *A.D. Tom Staebler, Kerig Pope*

fiat & associates
312 464 0964 *
312 554 1729 *

j o h n   k l e b e r

martha productions inc
310 390 9744
310 390 3161 *

the mccann company
214 526 2252
214 526 5565 *

* fax

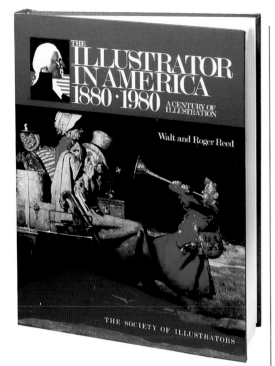

THE ILLUSTRATOR IN AMERICA
(1880-1980) -355 pp.
Compiled by leading authorities on illustration.
Contains 700 illustrations by 460 artists.
$40.00

ILLUSTRATED BOOKS

Drawing on its position as a resource of information and art, both past and present, the Society has created these two special volumes. One is the leading historical compendium of this artform and the other is the most powerful statement to date by illustrators addressing ecoloogy.

ART FOR SURVIVAL
248 pp, full color, 150 images
by contemporary illustrators commenting on the
Environment. Introductions by Tom Cruise
and others. $40.00

Society of Illustrators
Museum Shop

The Society of Illustrators Museum of American Illustration maintains a shop featuring many quality products. Four-color, large format books document contemporary illustration and the great artists of the past. Museum quality prints and posters capture classic images. T-shirts, sweatshirts, hats, mugs and tote bags make practical and fun gifts.

The Museum Shop is an extension of the Society's role as the center for illustration in America today. For further information or quantity discounts, contact the Society at
TEL: (212) 838-2560 / FAX: (212) 838-2561

ILLUSTRATED CALENDAR

Tapping the rich visual history of the Society's PERMANENT COLLECTION, this calendar is a sampler of sytlyes and subjects.

1994 CALENDAR
24 PP., Color. the 12 images feature Lyman Anderson, N.C. Wyeth, Norman Rockwell, Bernie Fuchs, Fred Otnes, Mead Schaeffer, Bob Peak and more. Printed on heavy, high-gloss paper with ample space to write in important dates.

SOCIETY OF ILLUSTRATORS • 128 East 63rd Street • New York, NY 10021

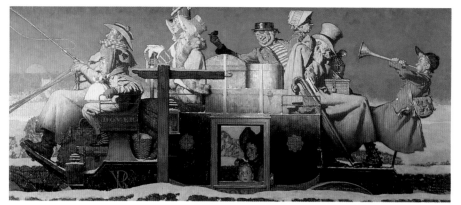

"The Dover Coach" by NORMAN ROCKWELL, 1935
$12.00

"Blond at a Filling Station" by MEAD SCHAEFFER, 1938
$12.00

"Horse Race" by HAROLD VON SCHMIDT, 1939
$12.00

MUSEUM QUALITY POSTERS

Posters of classic works from the Society's permanent collection.
Reproduced on glossy stock in a 20" x 30" format.
Suitable for framing. $12.00 per poster; $38.00 for the set of four.

"The Blue Cloak" by LYMAN ANDERSON
$12.00

EXHIBITION POSTERS

Posters created for exhibitions in the Society of Illustrators Museum of American Illustration. Suitable for framing. $10.00 per poster; $27.00 for the set of three.

"Recycled Ideas"
"The Illustrator and the
Environment "
by FOLON $10.00

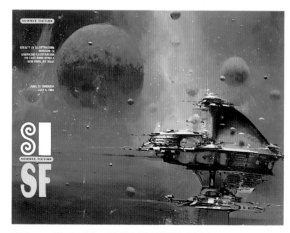

"Science Fiction" by JOHN BERKEY, 1984
$10.00

"Wizard of Oz", The Original Art by EDWARD SOREL, 1991
$10.00

EXHIBITION CATALOGS

These volumes have been created for exhibitions in the Society of Illustrators Museum of American Illustration. They focus on specific artists, eras or subjects.

COBY WHITMORE
20 PP., Color.
The good life of the 1950s and 1960s as illustrated in the Ladies Home Journal McCall's and Redbook.
$16.00

AMERICA'S GREAT WOMEN ILLUSTRATORS
(1850-1950)
24 pp, B&W.
Decade by decade essays by important historians on the role of women in illustration.
$5.00

NEW EDITION

150 pages in full color of Children's books from 1992. This volume contains valuable "how-to" comments from the artists as well as a publishers directory. A compilation of the exhibition, "The Original Art 1992 - Celebrating the Fine Art of Children's Book Illustration."
$29.95

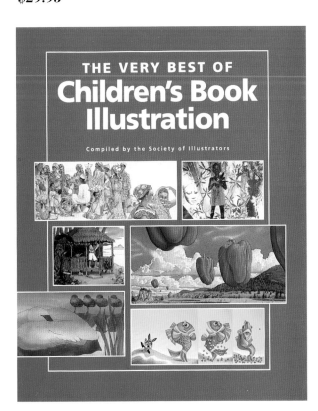

THE BUSINESS LIBRARY

Each of thesee volumes is a valuable asset to the professional artist whether established or just starting out. Together they form a solid base for your business.

The set of three volumes. $42.00

GRAPHIC ARTISTS GUILD HANDBOOK PRICING AND ETHICAL GUIDELINES - Vol. 7
Includes an outline of ethical standards and business practices, as well as price ranges for hundreds of uses and sample contracts.
$22.95

THE LEGAL GUIDE FOR THE VISUAL ARTIST
1989 Edition.
Tad Crawford's text explains basic copyrights, moral rights, the sale of rights, taxation, business accounting and the legal support groups available to artists.
$18.95

HEALTH HAZARDS MANUAL
A comprehensive review of materials and supplies, from fixatives to pigments, airbrushes to solvents.
$9.95

GIFT ITEMS

The Society's famous Red and Black logo, designed by Bradbury Thompson, is featured on the following gift items:

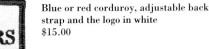

SI LAPEL PINS
$6.00
Actual Size

SI BASEBALL CAPS
Blue or red corduroy, adjustable back strap and the logo in white
$15.00

SI PATCH
White with blue lettering and piping - 4" wide
$4.00

SI TOTE BAGS
Heavyweight, white canvas bags are 14" high with the two-color logo
$15.00

SI CERAMIC COFFEE MUGS
Heavyweight 14 oz. mugs are white with the two-color logo
$6.00 each, $20.00 for a set of 4

SI T-SHIRTS

Incorporating the Society's logo in three designs (large SI, words and lines, multiple logo). Orange shirts with black lettering. Blue shirts with white lettering. White shirts with two color lettering.
$10.00 each.
SIZES: Small, Large, X-Large, XX-Large.

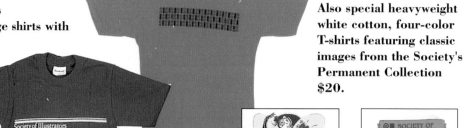

Also special heavyweight white cotton, four-color T-shirts featuring classic images from the Society's Permanent Collection $20.

"Easter" by
J.C. LEYENDECKER
The Saturday
Evening Post
1934

"The Black Arrow"
by N.C. WYETH
Frontispiece for the
Scribner's Classic by
Robert Louis Stevenson

SI SWEATSHIRTS

Blue with white lettering of multiple logos. Grey with large red SI.
$20.00 each.
Sizes:
Large,
X-Large,
XX-Large.

SI NOTE CARDS

Norman Rockwell greeting cards, 3-7/8" x 8-5/8", inside blank, great for all occasions.
Includes 100% rag envelopes

10 cards - $10.00
20 cards - $18.00
50 cards - $35.00
100 cards - $60.00

ORDER FORM
Mail to the attention of:
The Museum Shop, SOCIETY OF ILLUSTRATORS, 128 East 63rd Street, New York, NY 10021

35

NAME _____

COMPANY_____

STREET_____

CITY_____

STATE_____ZIP _____

DAYTIME PHONE ( ) _____

Enclosed is my check for $ _____
Make checks payable to Society of Illustrators
Please charge my credit card:
❏ American Express   ❏ Master Card   ❏ Visa
Card Number _____

Signature _____ Expiration Date _____

*please note if name appearing on the card is different than the mailing name.

Qty	Description	Size	Color	Price	Total

# of items ordered	Total price of item(s) ordered	
	*Shipping/handling per order	3.50
	TOTAL DUE	

*Foreign postage additional

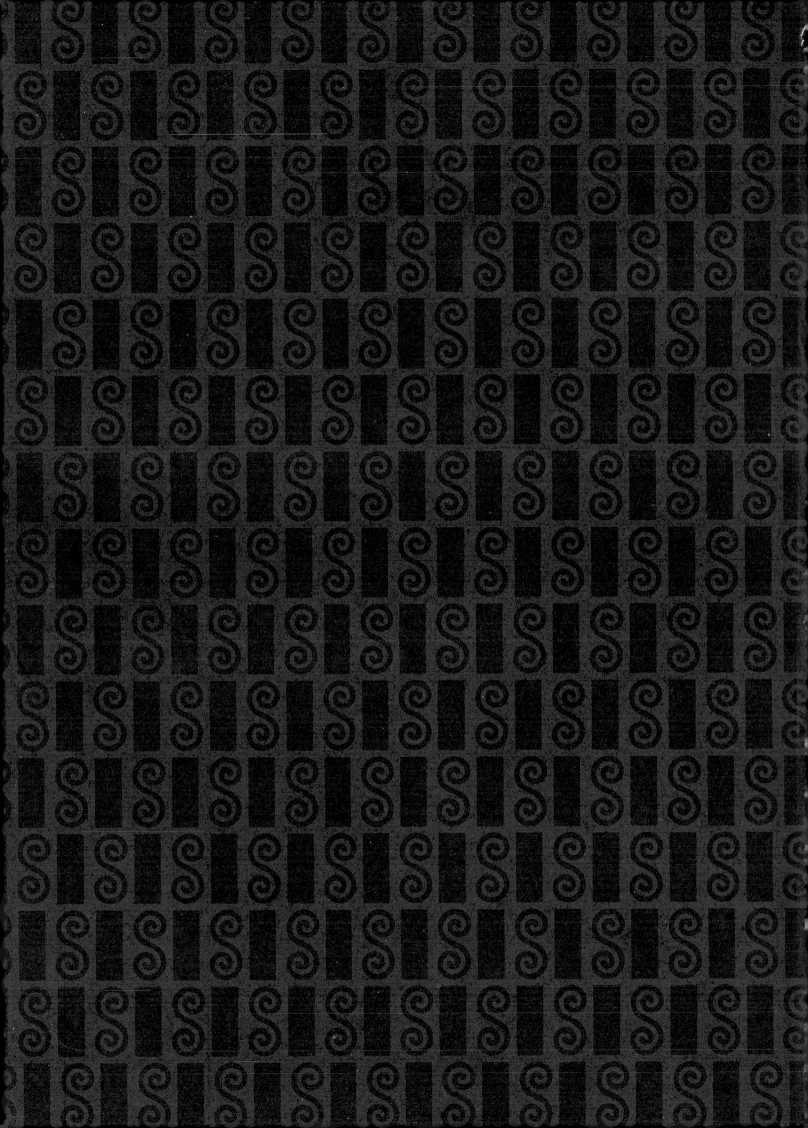